MIGRATION
AND DEVELOPMENT NEXUS
in the Princely State Tripura
(1900-1949)

DR. NILANJAN DE

Notion Press Media Pvt Ltd

No. 50, Chettiyar Agaram Main Road,
Vanagaram, Chennai, Tamil Nadu – 600 095

First Published by Notion Press 2021
Copyright © Dr. Nilanjan De 2021
All Rights Reserved.

ISBN

Hardcase: 978-1-68563-939-6
Paperback: 978-1-68563-908-2

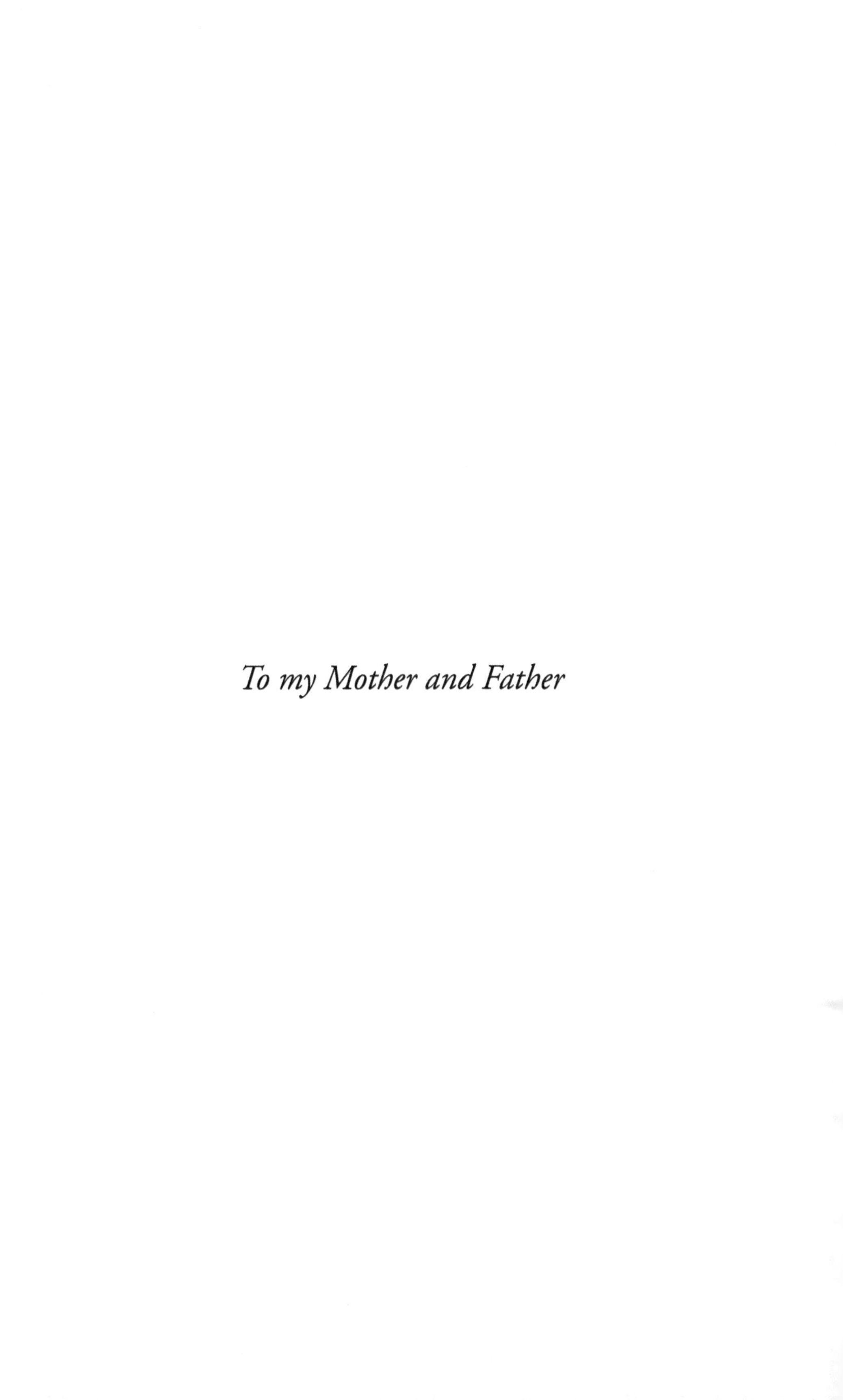

To my Mother and Father

Table of Contents

Preface

Tripura was one of those native states of India, which almost readily agreed to merge in the Indian Union in the wake of independence. However, until 14 October 1949, Tripura was a Princely State and thereafter it was integrated with the Indian Union as a Part "C" State under the direct administrative control of the Government of India. During the last fifty years (1900 – 1949) of Manikya rule in Tripura, a large number of immigrants entered Tripura from colonial India. However, the development process, which was initiated by the rulers of Tripura in the last quarter of the 19th century, got momentum in this period. Hence, the period witnessed both the dramatic change in the demographic structure of the state as well as its material development.

The development of a state cannot be confined only into its economic arena but socio-political as well as cultural fields of a state were also needed to be developed and modernized. Among the various guiding forces behind the development process of a state, migration often plays a vital role in it. A large number of immigrants while can destroy the socio-political and economic infrastructure of a state, at the same time it can provide a new dimension towards modernisation. Therefore, it becomes necessary to find out the relations between migration and the material development of Tripura from a historical perspective. In addition, how much migration is responsible for changing the total infrastructural change of the Princely state Tripura and what were the factors that worked behind the immigration also arose questions and this book is a humble attempt in this direction. I tried my best to scrutinize analytically the whole episode of migration during the last half of the Manikya rulers of Tripura and reveal the real picture out of it. I hope that the young scholars and researchers will find it informative and interesting, and the lovers of demographic study will receive incentives to the further research.

In this regard, I gladly express my sincere thanks to Mr. Sunil Krishna Paul, retired T.C.S. Officer (1995) and former Assistant Survey Officer (North and South district of Tripura) in 1971, Dharmanagar, for providing me valuable information and documents.

I give my heartfelt thanks to the Librarian and the staff of the Tribal Research and Cultural Institute for giving me access to the materials required for preparing this dissertation. I do acknowledge the help and kindness of many authorities, organizations, institutions and individuals. The most important of them are Education Directorate, Govt. of Tripura, Tripura State Museum, Tripura State Archives, Birchandra State Central Library, K.K. Handique Library, Gauhati University, District Library, Guwahati, Lakshminath Bezbaroa Central Library, Guwahati, various Public Libraries of the sub-divisions of Tripura, Assam University Central Library, Silchar.

I also acknowledge my indebtedness to all those, whose work I have consulted, referred to and quoted.

I thank the Almighty and my parents for their blessings and constant encouragement and finally I am grateful to my wife, brother, sister, sister in law, father in law, mother in law and to my little daughter Shatarupa, those who have extended their full cooperation to do my research project. Without their blessings and unending support, the work would have never been accomplished.

Finally, I acknowledge Notion Press for their untiring efforts in publishing the book.

Karimganj, Assam

Nilanjan De

4th October 2021

Chapter I

Introduction

Tripura is a small charming hill state, situated in the eastern part of India. It covered an area of 10,477, sq. km. It lies between $91^0 10'$ and $92^0 21'$ East longitude and $22^0 56'$ and $24^0 32'$ North Latitude. It is encircled by Bangladesh on three sides with long open borders of 839 km. Its only nexus with the Indian Union is simply in its northeastern border where roughly 162 km of its opening forms a boundary line partly in the north with the Karimganj district of Assam and partly in the east with Mizoram. On the other side of its border, it was encircled by the districts of Bangladesh like Sylhet, Comilla, Noakhali, and the Chittagong Hill Tracts respectively. However, there was a time when the States' territories stretched from the Sundarbans in the West and Burma in the East and South and Kamrup in the North.[1]

The name Tripura is a mysterious one, for the reason that, various scholars have given various opinions regarding the name. Some of the scholars opined that the name Tripura came from the name of goddess *Tripura Sundari* of *Radhakishorepur* while others considered it as a plagiaristic form of *Tri Puram*, meaning land of three cities. Kailash Chandra Singha, a chronicler of the Tripura Rajas, opined that Tripura is a corrupt form of *Tui-pra*, which means land adjoining water. The land probably bears the name Tripura because of its closeness to the water, for "it is a fact that in days of yore the boundaries of Tripura extended up to the Bay of Bengal when its rulers held sway from the Garo Hills to Arakan … It is relevant to

---

1   Dipak Kumar Choudhuri, *Reflection on the History of Tripura*, Kalyanbrata Chakraborty on behalf of Bhasa, Agartala, January, 2006, p.1.

note that even today the hill people pronounce the word as Tipra and not Tripura."[2] Indeed, the Tripura tribes are not familiar with any common term to assign their tribe and thus it seems still more probable that the word Tripura has its origin in the two significant words of the land, *tui* and *pra*.

However, the British Government named the territory 'Hill Tipperah', to demarcate the territory from the neighbouring 'Tipperah' (Comilla), which was one of the districts of Colonial India in the lower plains of East Bengal. Nevertheless, in the year 1920, the British Government replaced the name 'Hill Tipperah' with 'Tripura', at the request of the Maharaja of Tripura.[3]

Tripura is a land of tribal and non-tribal people but the aborigines of the state were tribes. Numerous tribal groups' organized the original dwellers of the state. At present, there are as many as nineteen tribes in Tripura, viz. 1) Lushai, 2) Mog, 3) Kuki including the following sub-tribes – i) Balte, ii) Belalhut, iii) Chhalya, iv) Fun, v) Hajong vi) Jangei, vii) Khareng, viii) Khepong, ix) Kuntei, x) Laifang, xi) Lentei, xii) Mizel, xiii) Namte, xiv) Pailu, xv) Rangchan, xvi) Rangkhole, xvii) Thangluya, 4) Chakma, 5) Garo, 6) Chaimal, 7) Halam, 8) Khasia, 9) Bhutia, 10) Munda including Kaur, 11) Orang, 12) Lepcha, 13) Santal, 14) Bhil, 15) Tripura of Tripuri (including Laskar), 16) Jamatia, 17) Noatia, 18) Reang, 19) Uchai.[4] Out of the nineteen tribes, five are the original tribes and they are viz. Tripuri, Noatia, Halam, Jamatia and Reang. The Mogs, Chakmas and Kukis came later. The Chakmas and the Mogs immigrated into Tripura from the Chittagong Hill Tracts and the Kukis immigrated from Lushai and Jaintia Hills. The rest of the non-indigenous tribes came mainly as tea garden labourers from Bihar, Orissa and Madhya Pradesh and ultimately settled here. The Tripuris were the most dominant tribe in the state and the ruling dynasty of Tripura belongs to this tribe.

---

2   *Tripura District Gazetteers*, Government of Tripura, Agartala, 1975, p. 1.

3   *Memoranda on the Indian State*, 1932, Government of India, Central Publication Branch, Calcutta, 1933, p. 220.

4   *Statistical Abstract of Tripura, 1964*, Statistical Department, Government of Tripura, Agartala, 1965, p.223.

Tripura though was an independent Princely State but from the 18th century onwards, she began to lose possession of her own territory. The rulers of Tripura were subdued by the Mughals in 1722 and were forced to cede the greater part of their plain territories known as 'Chakla Roshnabad' and pay tributes for the retention of the rest. Thus Tripura, so long a mighty kingdom covering a wide area, gently submerged into mere forgetfulness by turning itself into a mere province within the Mughal Empire. However, the British policy towards Tripura was to some extent different from the general feudatory policy of Mughal rule.

The English East India Company came to be in possession of Chakla Roshnabad under the grants from Nawab Mirzafar and Mirkasim, which was eventually included and confined in the *Dewani,* granted to the Company by the Mughal Emperor Shah Alam in 1765 A.D. Interestingly when the British came into contact with Tripura they found a peculiar form of Government as well as administration existing in Tripura. The whole territory of the state was divided into two parts – the hills and the plains. In the hill, the ruler was independent, but in the plains, which were known a 'Chakla Roshnabad', the ruler was mere a Zamindars under the Nawab of Bengal.

Therefore, during the colonial rule, Tripura remained divided into two parts – the hills –, which was commonly called by the British as 'Hill Tipperah' (after 1920 as Tripura) and the 'Chakla Roshnabad'. According to the Traverse Survey of the Survey Department, Chakla Roshnabad covers an area of 533.77 square miles.[5] The *Zamindari* of Chakla Roshnabad enclosed the vast areas of the districts of Tipperah (Comilla), Noakhali and Sylhet of the then Colonial Bengal.[6]

---

5   J.G.Cumming, I.C.S. Settlement Officer, *Survey and Settlement of the Chakla Roshnabad Estate in the Districts of Tippera and Noakhali, 1892-99.* Tripura State Tribal Cultural Research Institute & Museum, Government of Tripura, Agartala, December, 1997, p. 2.

6   *Census Bibarani* 1340 T.E. (1931 A.D), Tribal Research and Cultural Institute, Government of Tripura, Agartala, 1997, Editorial column.

Tripura continued to be a Princely State until it merged into the Union of India on 15th October 1949. However, after the partition of India in 1947, the Zamindari of Chakla Roshnabad went into the hand of erstwhile East Pakistan and the land of Tripura was confined only in the hilly region. From the Independence of India and her partition (15th August 1947) to the amalgamation of Tripura with the Indian Union (15th October 1949) the period of two years were considered as the 'Period of Regency'. During this first half of the 20th century, Tripura witnessed a massive flow of migrants from East Bengal and later East Pakistan.

After discussing the geographical and political structure of Tripura it becomes necessary to know about what is migration and what are the various aspects of migration. Migration is commonly known as the displacement of a person who leaves their place of birth or residence for another place. According to the United Nations Multilingual Demographic Dictionary, migration is a form of geographical or spatial mobility between one geographic unit and another, generally involving a change in residence from the place of origin or departure to the place of destination or arrival. In the sociological perspective, migration has been defined as the more or less, permanent movement of individuals or groups across symbolic or political boundaries into new residential areas and communities. Most of the sociological synopsis starts with Ravenstein's seven laws of migration.

The academic and historical perspective of migration can be explained through sociological analysis which is possible through the principal categories of migration theories like the neoclassical macro-economic theory, the new economics of migration, dual labour market or segmented labour market theory, world-system theory which is copied form of the Marxist approach to international migration, network migration, the theory of cumulative causation and the demographic principles of migration. The Marxist authors like Beard, Gorz, Castles and Kosack, Miles, Bovenkerk, Nikolinakos etc. argues that the class-based political course of action and the economic factors outline the migration policies. According to them, Migration is the direct consequence of inequalities that result from the process of capital accumulation and class differences, within and among nations.

In the migration study, especially in the international field of migration, there are various terms, which are used simultaneously, and interchangeably, viz. migrant, refugee, displayed person and asylum seeker.

The Migrants often makes a conscious choice to come to the host country. The refugee generally don't have any idea about their destination. Refugees are those people who were forced to leave their countries because they have been persecuted and were the victims of the situation.

A displaced person is a person who has been forced to leave his or her native place. The term refugee is also commonly used as a synonym for the displayed person. But the difference between these two terms is that the person who crossed the international border due to external pressure or force is called a displaced person while after crossing an international border due to external pressure or force and falls under one of the relevant international legal instruments is considered a refugee. Thus, we can say that a displaced person after his/her legal recognition by the host country is considered a refugee.

Asylum seekers are such migrants who have the power to choose their destination and got their recognition in the host country. The difference between the refugee and the asylum seeker is that the refugees are the people who are at risk of being persecuted by the host country while the asylum seekers have no such chance because they have their recognition in that host country.

Now after discussing various aspects of migration it is necessary to know migration from its historical perspective. Man has been a mobile creature ever since his emergence and thus the trend of migration is experienced by the human race for ages. The present distribution of the human population over the world is the outcome of that trend of migration. The modern history of international migration is generally divided into four periods – viz. mercantile period (1500 – 1800), industrial period, period of limited migration and post-industrial migration. In the mercantile period, world migration was dominated by flows out of Europe and stemmed from colonization and economic growth under mercantile capitalism. In this period, the Europeans came to inhabit large portions of America, Africa and Asia. However, the exact numbers of migrants are unknown but the European migrants indeed dominate the large parts of the world. The industrial period of migration begins in the 19th century and stemmed from industrial development in Europe and the spread of capitalism to former colonies in the New World.[7] During the period of industrialization in Europe, a large scale of migration occurred. The last part of this period, generally known as the period of economic globalization was characterized by huge flows of a human beings. In the initial stage of globalization, the European migrants generally choose the European colonies, "that were themselves in the throes of rapid industrialization and development. The United States by itself absorbed around 60% of Europe's total outflow and another 25% of the emigrants were scattered among Argentina, Australia, Canada and New Zealand"[8].

The next important period is the 'period of limited migration'. Due to the outbreak of World War I and II, the migration rate all over the world was decreased. The chauvinistic restrictions imposed by the various countries and the Great Depression of the 1930s virtually stopped all the movements. The movement that occurred during World War II was "largely of refugees and displaced persons and was not tied strongly to the rhythms of economic growth and development".[9] In the post-industrial period of migration, we find a rapid growth of migration worldwide. Migration now became a global phenomenon and its scope became truly global. Since 1960 Europeans have comprised an increasingly smaller fraction of world immigration flows and emigration from Africa, Asia and Latin America has

---

7   As quoted from Douglas, S. Massey, *Patterns and Process of International Migration in the 21st century,* Paper presented for Conference on African Migration in Comparative Perspective, Johannesburg, South Africa, June 2003, p. 1.

8   *Ibid.* p. 3.

9   *Ibid.*

increased dramatically. The variety of destination countries has also grown viz. Germany, France, Belgium, Switzerland, Sweden and the Netherlands. During the 1970s, even long-term countries of emigration such as Italy, Spain, and Portugal began receiving immigrants from the Middle East and Africa. After the rapid growth of oil prices in 1973 several less developed but capital-rich nations in the Persian Gulf also began to sponsor massive labour migration as well. By the 1980s, international migration spread in Asia, not just to Japan but also to newly industrilised countries such as Korea, Taiwan, Hong Kong, Singapore, Malaysia and Thailand.[10]

From the Indian perspective, an image of migration is rather different. The 20th century India witnessed three phases of migration viz. – i) during the period of Independence and the partition, especially from 1947 – 1952, ii) migration from 1952 – 1971, iii) migration from 1971 till date.

The persons who have migrated from the East as well as from West Pakistan to India are considered refugees. Nevertheless, the definition of refugees as given by the 1951 Convention of Refugees is not relevant in the case of refugees of post-partitioned India. The migrants from 1947 to 1952 were considered as the 'Old Migrants'. During 1964-65, a huge number of refugees came to India due to the communal riots in Khulna and Dacca and the flows continued as the Indo – Pak war broke out in 1965. Moreover, those people were truly refugees and not migrants. This flows of refugees from East Pakistan continued until 1971.

The international migrants or the refugees are not generally acknowledged by the host country, but it was a surprising event in world history that the migrants were welcomed by the small princely state of Tripura. It is evident that in the 19th century and before the amalgamation in the 20th century the migrants especially the Bengali people entered Tripura from Bengal and settled there after getting the royal patronage. The kings of Tripura welcomed the Bengali immigrants and patronized them for their valuable contributions to the various fields of administration and for their

---

10 *Ibid.* p. 4.

contribution to the economic development of the State through recovering and bringing more and more lands under plough cultivation. Accordingly, Tripura became a place of endurance for the landless Bengali peasants of undivided India. It is therefore natural that a large number of Bengali migrants entered Tripura for easy settlement.

The movements of immigrants were not a new phenomenon for the state of Tripura. Tripura began to witness the flow of immigrants' rights from the last quarter of the 19th century and before her amalgamation, she witnessed a large number of immigrants especially from Colonial Bengal immigrated into the state in search of jobs and livelihood. Moreover, due to the smooth association between the Colonial Bengal and Hill Tipperah, there was an excellent arrangement of socio-economic interaction, which started in the last part of the 19th century and carried on up to its merger with the Indian Union. This close affinity between the Colonial Bengal and Hill Tipperah caused the movements of the people from one place to another.

Maharaja Radha Kishore Deb Manikya was the ruler of Tripura when this hilly region put her step in the 20th century. The last part of the Manikya dynasty of Tripura witnessed the emergence of a new culture in Tripura, which was the outcome of the migration from the Colonial Bengal and from the adjoining territories of Hill Tipperah.

Whether the rulers of Tripura whole-heartedly wanted to make a close affinity with Colonial Bengal is a matter of long discussion, but they indeed had to admit the Bengalis into their territory to run the administration and other services. To modernize the administrative system, revenue, judiciary etc. the ruler of Tripura was totally dependent on the educated intelligentsia of Colonial Bengal provinces. In addition, the rulers of Tripura, to extent plough cultivation and to increase the land revenue encouraged the Bengali cultivators of the neighbouring British districts to immigrate into the State. The *Jangalabadi* system introduced by the ruler of Tripura also encouraged the Bengali cultivators of the adjoining territories to immigrate to Tripura.

In Tripura, the people who penetrated before the independence cannot be considered refugees. Based on the documents like Tripura State

Gazette Sankalan, 1903-1949, Statistical Account of Bengal, Vol.VI, by W.W.Hunter, Somendrachandra Deb Barma, Census Bibarani, 1341 T.E.(1931), Census Report 1310 T.E. (1901), they are truly economic migrants as they settled there to fulfil their economic interests. The people who entered the state after independence and its amalgamation with the Indian Union are considered as the displayed person or the refugees. The term migrant was also used by the Government of Tripura. However, according to the Census reports of India and different Refugee Registration Acts in India[11] those immigrants can be considered as refugees.

Hence, we observed two phases of migration in Tripura in the first half of the 20th century, which not only increased the number of populations of the state but also altered substantially the ethnic composition of Tripura's population and the resource use pattern.

The aborigines of the state began to be outnumbered by the immigrants' settlers, especially by the Bengali immigrants. However, the developmental process, which was initiated by the rulers of Tripura in the last quarter of the 19th century, got momentum in this period. Hence, the period witnessed both the dramatic change in the demographic structure of the state as well as its material development.

The development of a state cannot be confined only into its economic arena but the socio-political, as well as cultural field of a state, were also needed to be developed and modernized. Among the various guiding forces behind the developmental process of a state, migration often plays a vital role in it. A large number of immigrants while can destroy the socio-political and economic infrastructure of a state, at the same time it can provide a new dimension towards modernisation.

---

11 The Registration of Foreigners Act, 1939, the Foreigners Act, 1946, and the Foreigners Order, 1948 are the primary documents dealing with the treatment of foreigners in India. Article 2 of the 1939 Registration of Foreigners Act defines a foreigner as "a person who is not a citizen of India." The Foreigners Act of 1946 and the Foreigners Order of 1948 also uses this definition of a "foreigner", especially the refugees.

Now the question arises, whether by the substantial alteration of the demography of the state witnesses any real development? Therefore, it becomes necessary to find out the relations between migration and the material development of Tripura from a historical perspective. In addition, how much migration is responsible for changing the total infrastructural change of the Princely state Tripura and what were the factors that functioned behind the immigration also arose questions which were also required to be investigated.

Chapter II

Migration-Development Nexus: A Theoretical Study

In the twentieth century, especially after World War II, there was a huge debate among scholars regarding the relationship between migration and development. Hence, it becomes necessary to know the real meaning of these terms.

Migration is a global phenomenon and it is experienced by human society for ages. Population dynamics, regional developments, social, economic and political push and pull factors and other issues like history and culture shape it. It reflects a human effort to survive in the most testing conditions both natural and artificial or man-made. It manipulated almost every aspect of a state.

Migration is commonly known as the displacement of a person who leaves his or her place of birth or residence for another place. But migration is defined by various studies in different ways. In the population studies, "Migration implies a permanent, or at least a semi-permanent, change in the place of residence of individuals from one location to another".[12] According to the United Nations Multilingual Demographic Dictionary, migration is "a form of geographical or spatial mobility between one geographic unit and another, generally involving a change in residence from the place of origin or departure to the place of destination or arrival", In the sociological

---

12 Mohammad Izhar Hassan, *Population Geography*, Rawat Publications, Jaipur, 2005, p. 281.

perspective, migration has been defined as the more or less, permanent movement of individuals or groups across symbolic or political boundaries into new residential areas and communities.[13] According to P. Boyle, K. Halfacree and V. Robinson, migration means crossing the boundary of a political or administrative unit for a certain minimum period.[14] However, Stephen Castles went much further and opined that "Migration means taking up residence for a certain minimum period – say 6 months or a year."[15] Thus due to these variations in the definitions of migration it is not possible to sketch a particular contour of migration. Such variations highlight the fact that there is nothing objective about definitions of migration: they are the result of state policies, introduced in response to political and economic goals and public attitudes.[16]

Apart from various causes of migrations like social, economic, political and environmental factors, migration depends on the perception and behaviour of individuals concerned. Peoples move from one place to other to accomplish their desired goal. Often peoples move about from their place of origin to their destination to increase their wages or to improve their status of living. However, sometimes they are bound to move from their place of origin due to social, political, economic, religious, ethnic and environmental forces and pressures. Thus, the movements of people are steered by different external and internal forces. These differences affect the overall migration process. From the sociological perspective, different causes of migration produce different consequences. A migrant can be a labour, slave, highly skilled person, refugee, job seeker, asylum seeker, displaced person, businessperson, an illegal migrant or some other reasons for moving. Thus considering the above variations of migration no single theory can provide a comprehensive explanation for the migration process and thus there is no common and accepted theoretical framework.

---

13 Marshal Gorden, *Dictionary of Sociology,* OUP, Oxford and New York, 1998, p. 415.
14 As quoted in Stephen Castles, *International Social Science Journal,* Vol. 52, 2000, p. 269.
15 Stephen Castles, *International Social Science Journal,* Vol. 52, 2000, p. 270.
16 *Ibid.*

Moreover, "social scientists don't approach the study of immigration from a shared paradigm, but from a variety of competing theoretical viewpoints fragmented across disciplines, regions and ideologies".[17]

Under these circumstances when there is no definite theory of migration it becomes really hard to assimilate it with a state evolutionary process of development. The nexus between migration and development hence become critical.

Now let's see what does development really mean. According to the Cambridge dictionary development means, "the process in which someone or something grows or changes and becomes more advanced." According to Business dictionary development means, "The process of economic and social transformation that is based on complex cultural and environmental factors and their interactions".[18] The Nobel prize-winner Amartya Sen, opined that development must be judged by its impact on people and not only by changes in their income but more generally in terms of their choices, capabilities and freedoms. He said we should be concerned about the distribution of these improvements, not just the simple average for a society.[19] Hence, the development of society means even distribution of all-around progress. Now it has become really interesting to observe how migration fit itself in the developmental process of a state.

There has been increasing acknowledgement in the past few decades concerning migration as an inner flow in the developmental route of a state. The topic of the association between migration and development is not a new one and from the 50s' of the twenty-first century, it became a burning issue for discussion among scholars. The scholars are found to be divided in their views regarding the question of the role of migration behind the

---

17 Massey, Douglas, Joaquin Arango, Graeme Hugo, Ali Kouaouci, Adela Pellegrimo and J. Edward Taylor, *An Evaluation of International Migration Theory: A North American Case*, Population and Development Review, Vol. 20, No. 4, December 1994, p. 700.

18 http://www.businessdictionary.com/definition/development.html

19 http://www.cgdev.org/blog/what-development

development. The pessimistic and optimistic ideas and thoughts of the scholars on migration and development nexus created a wave of confusion and in this wave of evolution of the migration-development nexus concept, we found four distinct ideas in the 2nd half of the 20th century.

Previously the scholars were very optimistic in their outlook and consider the migration development nexus from a simple cost-benefit point of view. But from this concept, the idea postulates that "the flow of emigrants and the accompanying brain drain are partly or wholly compensated for by a reverse flow of money, ideas and knowledge"[20]. In the first phase i.e. from 1950s to **1960s** we find that the scholars are very much enthusiastic to relate remittances and return as a guiding force behind migration and development nexus. Their view "corresponded to overall economic modernization concepts in development thinking and to a belief that state capacity could shape economic growth as well as control migration according to national needs".[21] The historical economist Charles P. Kindleberger propagated ideas linking development to migrants' return to their home countries and lauded capital and knowledge transfers that would initiate development take-off.[22]

The second phase of the study i.e. from the 1960s and 1980s is dominated by Marxist researchers and was influenced by the World system theory of migration. This theory is a macro-sociological perspective that seeks to explain the dynamics of the capitalist world economy as a total social system.[23] Immanuel Wallerstein is one of the chief exponents of this theory. According to this theory, migration is caused by sectoral and institutional imbalances between three distinct geographical zones – the core, the

---

20   Thomas Faist, Margit Fauser, and Peter Kivisto (ed), *The Migration-Development Nexus: A Transnational Perspective*, Palgrave Macmillan, UK, 2011, p.5

21   *Ibid.*

22   Mattis Hennings, *The Migration and Development Nexus: A Case Study of Jordan since the 1950s*, The University of North Carolina at Chapel Hill, March 24, 2013. p.13

23   Carlos A. Martinez Vela, *World System Theory*, ESD. 83 – Fall 2001, p. 1.

semi-periphery and periphery.[24] They consider that there is no relation between migration and development and often speculating the opposite relationship: that migration arose from a condition of underdevelopment and they were concerned with the ideas of brain drain and dependency.[25]

In this phase another important Mobility transition theory of Zelinsky immerged. The fundamental idea of Zelinsky's hypothesis i.e. there is a fundamental, but complex and non-linear relationship between the occurrence of specific forms of migration and more general socio-economic and demographic development processes is an empirically more realistic hypothesis than neoclassical models.[26]

In the 1990s, the migration scholars like Douglas Massey highlighted various shortcomings of those earlier studies regarding their theoretical understanding and methodological approaches in migration and development nexus. He criticised those incomplete analyses of the migration development nexus. Hence, in this period we find a careful optimistic analysis of migration development nexus and handsomely presenting migration as an agent of the developmental process. But the scholars of the present day tried to detect the prime force beneath the nexus. They assume that the relationship between migration and development is linear and positive, i.e. that migration necessarily contributes positivity to development and that is by the way of remittances. However, scholars like Hein De Hass is not ready to accept it rather, according to him the relationship between migration and development is reciprocal.

Hence, it is clear that a real controversy remains regarding the nature of the nexus between migration and development. It creates confusion between the nature of migration and the developmental process of the host

---

24 Chandan Nandy, *Illegal Immigration from Bangladesh to India: The emerging conflicts,* Slifka Program in Inter-Communal Coexistence, Brandeis University, November 30, 2005, p.7.

25 Mattis Hennings, *Op.cit.* .14

26 Hein de Haas, *Migration And Development A Theoretical Perspective,* International Migration Institute, James Martin 21st Century School, University of Oxford, Year 2008, Paper 9, p. 13.

country. Whether underdevelopment factor is responsible for migration of those countries or development of those migrants in the host country is responsible for its development is not clear in each and every scenario of migration development nexus and if it is in the case like Tripura then it becomes really tough to decipher the real connection between migration and development.

Therefore, to understand the migration and development nexus in Tripura it is necessary to understand first the nature of migration that occurred in Tripura during the period of our study.

Chapter III

Migration and Demographic Change in Tripura

There was close socio-economic contact between the colonial Bengal and the princely hilly state Tripura and this close attraction developed due to this political symmetry, which was associated with the geographical area. Tripura's fate was shaped by this close connection throughout the late 19th century until the independence of India in 1947. The pattern of this interaction was dictated by the policy of the British in favour of modernization so that Tripura could serve the imperial interest.

Furthermore, this close affinity between the Colonial Bengal and Hill Tipperah instigated the movements of the people from one place to another. The flow of migration, which was started in the last part of the 19th century, continued up to the independence of India.

The last part of the Manikya dynasty of Tripura witnessed the emergence of a new culture in Tripura, which was the outcome of the migration from the Colonial Bengal and from the adjoining territories of Hill Tipperah. The nature of migration in Tripura was administrative, political, religious, social and economic.

The rulers of Tripura enthusiastically wanted to make a close affinity with Bengal because they had to admit the educated Bengalis into their territory to run their administration and other services and to satisfy the British requirements.

The first Imperial census of Tripura was started in 1872. The following table indicates the population growth in Tripura from 1872 to 1901 A.D.

Table 3.1.

Population in Tripura (Hill Tipperah) in the closing decades of the 19th century.

Year	Total population	Total increase	Increase in Percentage
1872	35,262	-	-
1881	95,637	+60,375	17.1%
1891	1,37,432	+41,805	44%
1901	1,73,325	+35,880	26%

Source: *Census Bibarani 1340 T.E.* (1931 A.D), Tribal Research and Cultural Institute, Government of Tripura, Agartala, 1997, Editorial column.

The first reliable census was that of 1901 according to which the number of inhabitants was 26 per cent more than ten years before."[27]

Accordingly, Tripura started its journey in the 20th century with a population of 1, 73,325. In the census of 1901, special interest was also given to find out the number of immigrants in Tripura. In the census of 1901 in Tripura, the Bengali people were once again divided into Hindu Bengali and Muslim Bengali. It was said in that census that the high caste Hindu and Muslim people are few in number. Tables no. 3.2 and 3.3 show the numbers of Hindu Bengalis and Muslim Bengali peoples of various social categories.

Table 3.2.

Bengali Hindu according to the Census of 1901

Caste	Number
Brahmins	678
Baidya	223
Kayasthas	1,704

---

27   *Census Bibarani 1340 T.E., op.cit*, p. 26

Sudra	1,003
Barai	690
Teli	677
Kamar	458
Napit	353
Yogi	2,014
Kapali	1,755
Namasudra	3,508
Kaiborta	746
Patni	703
Saha	279
Dhopa	281
Total No.	15,072

Source: *Census Report 1310 T.E. (1901 A.D.)*, Tribal Research Institute, Government of Tripura, Agartala, Re-printing 1995, pp.21-22.

Table 3.3.

Bengali Muslim according to the Census of 1901

Caste	Number
Kaji	34
Mughal	30
Sayyed	98
Pathen	29
Sheik	44,426
Total	44,617

Source: *Census Report 1310 T.E. (1901 A.D.)*, Tribal Research Institute, Government of Tripura, Agartala, Re-print 1995, p. 22.

From the Table No. 3.2 and 3.3 it is clear that the total number of Bengali people living in Tripura in the year 1901 was 59,689. It was enumerated that 43,894 people migrated to Tripura[28] though in the Imperial Gazetteers of India Vol XIII the numbers of immigrants were 40,000.[29] According to J. B. Ganguli, those migrated people came to Tripura from the neighbouring districts of Bengal.[30] Those immigrants were migrated mostly from the Sylhet district of Assam and from Tipperah, Noakhali and Chittagong and table 3.4, makes it clear that most of those migrants are from Sylhet and Tipperah i.e. the main part of them were Bengali migrants.

Table 3.4.

Immigrants in Tripura in 1901 census

Source of Migration	1901
Tipperah	12,055
Noakhali	4,146
Chittagong	6,272
Chittagong Hill Tracts	1,228
Central Provinces and States	160
United Provinces and States	988
Assam * (Sylhet)	16,106
Elsewhere	2939
Total immigrant population	43,894

Source: 1. *Census of Insdia, 1901, Vol.VI, The Lower Provinces of Bengal and their feudatories,* Part I, The Report, Bengal Secretariat Press, Calcutta, 1902, Appendix I, p. vi.

2. *Census Bibarani 1340 T.E.* (1931 A.D), Tribal Research and Cultural Institute, Government of Tripura, Agartala, 1997, p.46.

The number of immigrants of the period constituted approximately 25.38 per cent of the total population. However, if we go through the sex ratio

---

28   Ibid, p.34.

29   *Imperial Gazetteers of India. Vol.XIII, op.cit.*

30   J.B.Ganguli, *The Benign Hills*, Tripura Darpan Prakashani, Agartala, March 1983, p. 8.

of the immigrants, then the real cause behind the migration can be found. Table 3.5 shows the sex ratio of the immigrants in Tripura, 1901.

Table 3.5.

Sex Ratio according to the census 1901.

Class	Male	Female
Bengali Hindu	8,997	6,079
Bengali Muslim	24,300	20,317
Total	33,297	26,396

Source: *Census Report 1310 T.E. (1901 A.D.)*, Tribal Research Institute, Government of Tripura, Agartala, Re-print 1995, p. 22.

From the above table, it is clear that the female percentage was lower than the male. This fact reveals that the people who migrated from Bengal to Tripura were moved by the easy earning in Tripura. The officials, government employees, farmers and the working class came to Tripura for employment only, not intending to settle in the State permanently and therefore, they left their family members at home. "The new comers do not at once entirely leave their residence in British territory, they keep their families and friends there, and make in Hill Tipperah only *Khamar Baris* or farm houses in which they live for the purposes of carrying on their cultivation."[31] Similarly W. W. Hunter in the *Statistical Account of Bengal*, Vol. VI, said, "Among the Bengalis, women are never employed in field labour, but the children occasionally take part in the work of cultivation."[32]

However, the physical features and the geographical dimension of Hill Tipperah not only attracted the Bengali immigrants but also the tribes and the Manipuris. The tribes who were considered as the modern immigrants in Tripura according to the Census Report of 1901 (1310 T.E.) were the

---

31 Annual Report on the General Administration of the Political Agency of Hill Tippera for the Year 1886, No-407, dated 7th July, 1887, para-34, Tripura Secretariat Archives, Bundle-51, Serial No-13 (un published).

32 W. W. Hunter, *Statistical Account of Bengal*, Vol. VI, London, 1876, p. 505. (1973 Reprint).

Chakmas and the Mogs. The numbers of the Chakmas, the Mogs and the Manipuris in the year 1901 are shown in table no 3.6.

Table 3.6.
Population of Chakma, Mog and the Manipuri in Tripura according to the Census 1901.

Name	Total Population	Male	Female
Chakma	4,510	2,432	2,078
Mog	1,491	771	720
Manipuri	12,851	6,765	6,096
Muslim Manipuri	405	195	210

Source: *Census Report 1310 T.E. (1901 A.D.)*, Tribal Research Institute, Government of Tripura, Agartala, Re-print 1995. p. 18.

The Chakma tribe was considered the modern immigrant tribe of Tripura according to the Census Report 1901 (1310 T.E.). In 1872, about 400 persons of the Chakma tribe emigrated from the Chittagong Hill Tracts and settled in the territory of the Tipperah Raja.[33] Their main occupation was *Jhum* cultivation and the state Tripura with her splendid opportunities of *Jhum* cultivation cordially acknowledged those Chakma immigrants in the territory. However, along with the attraction of fertile lands for *Jhum* cultivation in Tripura, the Chakmas of the Chittagong Hill Tracts were forced to leave their own homeland.

The Mogs were also considered as the immigrant tribes of Tripura. It was considered that the Mogs migrated to Tripura from Arakan due to some political disturbances. The Mogs were also considered as the modern tribes of Tripura and in 1901, though they were very few in number.

The Manipuris migrated into Tripura chiefly from Cachar and Sylhet. When the civil war started in the Manipur State, some of the Manipuris entered into Cachar and Sylhet, and from those places, they migrated into

---

33 W. W. Hunter, op. sit. 492-93

Tripura.[34] In addition, the rulers of both the state maintained a cordial relation among themselves and matrimonial relations between the two royal families accelerated the migration process.

It is clear from the census report of 1901 that the migration already started in Tripura in the last quarter of the 19th century. This trend of migration continued in the first half of the 20th century until its merger with the Indian Union and the nature of migration in that period was also different. Although economic push-pull factors were the guiding force behind the migration the changing political scenario of Colonial India due to spontaneous movement for freedom organized by the Indian National Congress, revolutionary activities and communal disturbances triggered the people to immigrate into the hilly princely state like Tripura.

In the first half of the 20th century i.e. before the merger with the Indian Union, five censuses took place in this Princely State. Table 3.7 shows the population of Tripura as depicted in those various censuses.

Table 3.7.

Population of Tripura according to various Census.

Year	Population	Decadal variation	% decadal variation
1901	1,73,325	–	–
1911	2,29,613	56,288	32.48
1921	3,04,437	78,824	32.59
1931	3,82,450	78,013	25.63
1941	5,13,010	1,30,560	34.14
1951	6,39,029	1,26,019	24.56

Source: Census of India 1961, Vol. XXVI, Tripura, District Census Handbook, Section – I, C.R.Paul, Government of Tripura, Government Printing and Stationary Department, Agartala, 1964, p. 35.

---

34 *Census Bibarani 1340 T.E, op.cit*, p. 96.

The table portrays that the flow of migrants continued after 1901 and the percentage of those migrants remained almost the same until 1921. However, the census report of 1931 depicts that the flow of migrants was reduced during the period from 1921 to 1931, though once again it increased enormously in the next decade (1931 to 1941).

It is also evident from the above table 3.8 that in the first thirty years of the 20th century in Tripura the decadal variation was almost the same. Now if we go through the number of the natural population in Tripura then we find that the number of natural population in Tripura increased quite satisfactorily. Table no. 3.8 portrays the number of natural population of the 1st three decades of the 20th century.

Table 3.8.
Natural population of Tripura (1901 – 1931)

	1901	1911	1921	1931
Real Population	1,73,325	2,29,613	3,04,437	3,82,450
No. of Immigrants	43,894	81,663	96,386	1,14,383
No. of Emigrants	152	1,372	358	6,543
Natural Population*	1,29,583	1,49,322	2,08,409	2,74,610

Source: *Census Bibarani 1340 T.E.* (1931 A.D), Tribal Research and Cultural Institute, Government of Tripura, Agartala, 1997, p.34

Immigration into Hill Tipperah in the 20th century was not confined among the Bengali migrants, but it also became a centre of attention for the various communities. As mentioned earlier that the Chakmas and the Mogs began to immigrate into Hill Tipperah in the 19th century and they continued their journey of immigrating into Tripura in the 1st half of the 20th century. Other than the Chakmas and the Mogs, the communities that were attracted towards Tripura during the period under review were *Santal, Munda, Garo, Bodo, Khasi, Kandra, Kurmi, Koch, Kora, Brinjhia, Kosta, Cachari,* Oraon etc. Among them *Santal, Munda, Oraon, Kanda, Kaur, Pan or Panika, Khandaet, Binjhia,* etc. Those communities were migrated from Bihar, Orissa, Madhya Pradesh and Madras. They were basically tea garden labourers.

Table no. 3.9 shows the number of tea gardens and their labourers in two specific census reports of 1921 and 1931.

Table 3.9.

Number of Tea gardens and their labourers (1921 & 1931 census)

Year	Men	Women	Total	No. of gardens
1921	2640	2365	5005	36
1931	2896	2555	5451	50

Source: *Census Bibarani 1340 T.E. (1931 A.D)*, Tribal Research and Cultural Institute, Government of Tripura, Agartala, Re-print 1997, p. 109.

The tea garden labourers after migrating from their place of origin viz. Bihar, Orissa, Bengal and Madhya Pradesh, settled down in Hill Tipperah permanently. Table 3.10 depicts the tribe name, number and the place of origin of those migrant tea garden labourers in the year 1931.

Table 3.10.

Distribution of immigrant tea garden labourers (1931).

Sl. NO	Name of Tribe	Hailing from	Population in 1931	Main Occupation
1	Oraon	Chotanagpur, Bihar	979	Tea garden labour
2	Kanda	Orissa	667	Tea garden labour & agriculture
3	Kaur	Chotanagpur, Bihar	117	Tea garden labour
4	Khandaet	Orissa	752	-Do-
5	Khaira	Chotanagpur, Bihar	133	Tea garden labour & agriculture

Continued...

6	Gareri	Bihar	58	Tea garden labour
7	Ghashi	Chotanagpur	90	-Do-
8	Turi	Chotanagpur	139	-Do-
9	Naia	Santal Pargana	37	-Do-
10	Nageshia	Chotanagpur	22	-Do-
11	Pan or Panika	Chotanagpur & Orissa	1064	Tea garden labour & agriculture
12	Binjhia	Chotanagpur	114	Tea garden labour*
13	Bhuia	Chotanagpur	139	-Do-
14	Bhumija	Orissa	452	Tea garden labour & agriculture
15	Munda	Chotanagpur	2058	-Do-
16	Lodha	Chotanagpur	37	-Do-
17	Santal	Santal Pargana	735	-Do-
Total			**7593**	

They were basically agriculturalists but in Tripura, they settled themselves as Tea garden labourers.

Source: *Census Bibarani 1340 T.E. (1931 A.D)*, Tribal Research and Cultural Institute, Government of Tripura, Agartala, Re-print 1997, pp.71-75

The Chakmas and the Mogs, the two modern immigrant tribes of Tripura as mentioned earlier, continued to immigrate into Tripura in the period under review. They forced the earlier settlers like Riang and Noatia to move further north to make space for them.[35] Table no. 3.11 shows the number of Chakmas from 1901 to 1931.

---

35   Bani Prasanna Misra, *op.cit*, p. 15.

Table 3.11.

Number of Chakma community (1901-1931).

Year	Number of Chakmas
1901	4510
1911	4310
1921	5738
1931	8730

Source: *Census Bibarani 1340 T.E.* (1931 A.D), Tribal Research and Cultural Institute, Government of Tripura, Agartala, Re-print 1997, pp.211, 229, 142 and 95.

Mogs, another immigrant tribe of Tripura continued their journey of emigrating from their place of origin to Tripura. The Mogs entered Tripura from the south and the majority of them settled themselves mainly into two sub-divisions like Belonia and Sabroom. The other areas where also they settled themselves during the period under review were Amarpur, Sonamura, and Udaipur. Table no. 3.12 depicts the number of Mogs in Tripura from the year 1901 to 1931.

Table 3.12.

Number of Mog community (1901-1931).

Year	Number of Mogs
1901	1,491
1911	1,930
1921	N.A
1931	5,748

N.A. – Not available.

Source: *Census Bibarani 1340 T.E.* (1931 A.D), Tribal Research and Cultural Institute, Government of Tripura, Agartala, Re-print 1997, p.p.211, 229 and 94

If both tables 3.11 and 3.12 are compared then it is found that, between 1901 and 1931, the Mog population increased very fast. Both are immigrant tribes and B. P. Misra opined, "they might have increased their number only by considerable migration."[36] The rulers of Tripura also encouraged those immigrants Mogs and provides them with every single facility to settle in Tripura. In the Administration Report of the Tripura State for 1934-35, it was mentioned that some of them were allotted lands in Bhatkhawri and Abhanga moujas. Moreover, it has been pointed out in the report that "The reclamation by the Mogs was very satisfactory, as a result of which the major portion of Bhatkhawri … has now turned into a small decent village."

As it is mentioned earlier that the Manipuri community migrated from the Cachar and Sylhet district of Assam in the 19th century and their number in Tripura, according to Census 1901 was 12,851 and Manipuri Muslims were 405. Later, their number began to increase and according to Census Bibarani 1340 T.E., in the year 1921 they were 15,549 and in the year 1931, the number was 19,210.[37] The exact number of Manipuri people in Tripura in the years 1911 and 1941 were not found but it was stated in the Imperial Table No. 10 in the Census Bibarani 1340 T.E. that, 16,381 people knew the Manipuri language in the year 1911 and among them 8,717 were men and 7,664 were women.[38]

Other than the tea garden labourers, the Chakmas, the Mogs and the Manipuris, the communities who migrated into Tripura in the period under review were – *Garo, Kandra, Kurmi, Koch, Kora, Kosta, Cachari, Kami, Kishan, Khawosh, Khas, Gurung, Gharti, Damai, Doshad, Nagar, Newar, Pashi, Baraake, Bind, Mangor, Majhi, Mahar, Rai, Rajput or Chatri, Rajowar, Limbu.* Those people came to Tripura from various parts of British India for their livelihood. Table 3.13 highlights their number, occupation in Tripura and their place of origin according to the Census Bibarani 1340 T.E. (1931).

---

36 Bani Prasanna Misra, *op.cit*, p. 17.

37 *Census Bibarani 1340 T.E. (1931 A.D)*, op.cit, pp. 142, 171.

38 Ibid. p.223.

Table 3.13.
Various small migrant communities in
Tripura according to Census 1931.

Community	Number	Occupation	Place of Origin
Garo	2143	Jhum cultivation	Garo Hills
Kandra	34	Day labour and watchmen	Orissa
Kurmi	338	Agriculture and domestic servant	Bihar
Koch	67	Agriculture	North Bengal
Kora	172	Earth cutting	Dravirian Origin
Kosta	1	Agriculture	Baleshwar
Cachari	4	-	Cachar district
Kami	2	Goldsmith and blacksmith	Darjeeling and Jalpaiguri
Kishan	29	-	Darjeeling
Khawash	25	-	Nepal
Khas	36	-	Darjeeling
Gurung	137	-	Darjeeling
Gharti	1	-	Darjeeling
Damai	17	Tailoring and singing	Darjeeling
Doshad	26	Labour	Bihar
Nagar	13	Agriculture	North Bihar
Newar	1	-	Nepal
Pashi	212	-	Bihar
Baraake	28	Weaver	Chotanagpur
Bind	282	Fishing	Bihar
Mangor	24	-	Nepal
Majhi	473	-	Darjeeling
Mahar	195	Preparing household goods	Orissa
Rai	3	-	Nepal

Continued...

Rajput or Chatri	30	-	North India
Rajowar	22	-	Bihar
Limbu	7	-	Darjeeling and Jalpaiguri

Source: *Census Bibarani 1340 T.E.* (1931 A.D), Tribal Research and Cultural Institute, Government of Tripura, Agartala, Re-print 1997. pp.69 – 75.

Another tribe of north east India who migrated into Tripura during this period under review were the Khasis. Their exact number was not found in any Government records. They migrated from the Khasi Hills of Meghalaya and from the borders of Assam.

Surprisingly, among the nontribal immigrants, the flow of Bengali Muslim immigrants in Tripura decreased considerably in the period under review. As it is pointed out earlier that the number of Bengali Muslims in Tripura was much more than the Bengali Hindus in Hill Tipperah according to Atish Chandra Choudhury's Census Report 1310 T.E. (1901 A.D.). However, if we go through table no. 3.14 then it becomes clear that the number of Bengali Muslims in Tripura decreased at a considerable rate.

Table 3.14.

Number of Bengali Muslims in Tripura (1901-51)

Census Year	Total population	Muslim Population	Variation in %
1901	1,73,325	45,323	26.15
1911	2,29,613	68,953	43.33
1921	3,04,437	82,288	26.68
1931	3,82,450	1,03,720	26.04
1941	5,13,010*	1,23,570**	19.14**
1951	6,45,707	1,36,981	21.21

Source: 1) *Census Bibarani 1340 T.E.* (1931 A.D), Tribal Research and Cultural Institute, Government of Tripura, Agartala, Re-print 1997 Editorial Column, Table No. 6.

2) Statistical Abstract of Tripura 1978, Directorate of Statistics and Evaluation, Government of Tripura, Agartala, 1981, p. 31.

*3) *Census of India 1961,* Vol. XXVI, Tripura, District Census Handbook, Section – I, C.R.Paul, Government of Tripura, Government Printing and Stationery Department, Agartala, 1964, p. 35.

** 4) Anjali Chakraborty, *Muslim Inhabitants of Tripura: A Demographic and Socio-Cultural Profile,* Folklore and Folkloristics, Vol.2; No.1, June 2009, p. 2.

The reason behind the diminution of the Muslim population in Tripura was due to the flow of an immense number of Hindu immigrants into Tripura, not only from the adjoining territories of the state but also from the other parts of India. As it is stated earlier that the people from Bengal immigrated much more in number than the other British states of India and the maximum number of Bengali immigrants were from the district of Tipperah and Sylhet. The trends of migration remain the same from the year 1901 to 1931. The tables (Table No. 3.15 & 3.16) portray a clear picture of the above statement.

Table 3.15.

Number of people immigrated into Tripura from various parts of India.

Source of Migration	1911	1921	1931
Bengal	48,042	46,061	67,946
Assam	27,506	36,978	33,262
Bihar, Orissa	2,002	5,077	4,153
Madras	1,046	2,675	2,166
Madhya Pradesh	1,432	2,227	1,341
United Province	1,281	1,685	2,116
Ajmer, Mewar	1	70	9
Punjab	50	44	80
Bombay	1	77	82
Other Native States of India	244	1,244	2,591

Source: *Census Bibarani 1340 T.E.* (1931 A.D), Tribal Research and Cultural Institute, Government of Tripura, Agartala, Re-print 1997, pp.43-44

Table 3.16.

Number of people immigrated into Tripura from various districts of Bengal and Assam

Source of Migration	1911	1921
Tipperah	35,002	25,689
Noakhali	4,759	4,583
Chittagong.	5,577	9,891
Hilly tracts of Chittagong.	105	1,469
Dacca	1,434	2,616
Sylhet	25,549	33,939
Lushai	760	1,434
Other districts of Assam	1188	1,608

Source: *Census Bibarani 1340 T.E.* (1931 A.D), Tribal Research and Cultural Institute, Government of Tripura, Agartala, Re-print 1997, p. 44

Another form of migration, which is evident in Tripura in the period under review, is the temporary migrants in the form of "Ziratia" peasants. Temporary migrants are those who used to leave their own country for a particular time span and return back to their own country after a specific or stipulated period.

In the second half of the nineteenth century India witnessed the growth of nationalism and the development of the sense of revenge against the British colonial rule in the form of a "nationalist movement". It reached its culmination in the first half of the twentieth century. The British Government also tried their best to restrain the growing "nationalist movement" in India, which they usually considered as "terrorist activities". The repressive measures of the British Government pushed the revolutionary activists to take shelter in a safe place and Hill Tipperah was one of the safe passages and safe places for shelter for those freedom fighters. In addition, Tripura became a place of the training centre for those revolutionary activists. Places like Belonia, Udaipur and in a tea garden at Kailashahar in Tripura where training centres were set up.[39]

A large number of members of the Anusilan Samity and Yugantar Organization came to Tripura not only for extending their activities but also for a safe shelter. A secret branch of the Anusilan Samity of Comilla group was established in 1931 at Raja Babu's House, Krishnanagar, Agartala under the leadership of Pravat Roy, Susil Deb Barma and Kanti Deb Barma. Another cell of Anusilan Samity was working at Narsing Akhra in Agartala under the leadership of Ananta De.[40] Moreover, a small group of workers of Kalyan Sangha, Brahmanbaria, which was a branch of Yugantar Organisation under Hem Ghosh and Lalit Barman, worked in this State since, 1928.[41] A number of the underground terrorists used to hide in the village of Dukhli, Pratapgarh etc., around the capital city of Agartala.[42] Those "revolutionary activists" were political migrants, though they migrated temporarily into Tripura.

Not only the 'revolutionary activists', but also in early 1921 several *Khilafatists* and non-co-operation agitators began to infiltrate into Tripura from the adjoining British districts of Tripperah, Noakhali, and Sylhet [43] to escape themselves from the atrocities of the British Government. Mr Sunil Krishna Paul, retired T.C.S. officer informed that among those revolutionary activists working in Tripura and *Khilafat*, non-cooperation and civil disobedience agitators, those who infiltrated in Tripura, many of them permanently settled in the state.[44]

Along with the social and economic push factors, the political and communal factors of British India were also responsible for immigration into Tripura. Tripura began to feel the atrocious impact of communal

---

39 *Tripura District Gazetteers,* op.cit. pp.120-121.

40 Tripur Chandra Sen, op. cit., p.56.

41 Ibid.

42 Gayatri Bhatacharyya, op. cit. p. 11.

43 *Tripura District Gazetteers, op.cit,* p.121.

44 Sunil Krishna Paul, retired T.C.S. Officer *interview* taken on 22nd May, 2016 and 20th Oct, 2016, respectively.

tension and political turmoil in British India culminating in the partition of India from a much earlier date.[45] The influx of migrants due to political and communal turmoil in Tripura began almost in 1942 when a great communal riot took place in Raipur P.S. in the district of Dacca.[46] Syama Prasad Mookerjee in his diary, dated 6th December 1945, mentioned that "Early in April, that is, a fortnight later, terrible devastation took place in the rural areas in the Narayangunge sub-division. Nearly eighty villages were burnt and looted; about 3000 people fled for their lives to the nation-State of Tippera. Hindus were about fifteen per cent here; Muslims fifty-five per cent. Leaflets were circulated that Hindus if they chose to live must live as converts to Islam. Fresh conversions took place."[47]

Subsequently, due to the communal chaos in response to the 'Direct Action Day' in the district of Noakhali and Chandpur, a large number of migrants came to Tripura in the year 1946 and this was the biggest influx of refugees in Tripura before the partition of India.[48] According to Tripur Chandra Sen, "several thousands of refugees came to Agartala"[49] due to the Noakhali riots. However, some of the migrants returned to their homes on the assurance given by Mahatma Gandhi, but the majority of them did not respond to it and settled in Tripura.[50]

Hence, we can say that during the period under study, the flow of immigration, which started in the last quarter of the 19th century, continued in the 20th century. Immigration became a major force in changing population scenario of Tripura during those decades. The immigrants completely changed the demographic pattern of the state. It appears that from almost all sections of the society, people immigrated to Tripura to

---

45 Pravas Ranjan Bhattacharjee, *Economic Transition in Tripura,* Vikas Publishing House Pvt. Ltd., New Delhi, p.48.

46 *Tripura District Gazetteers, op.cit.* p. 137.

47 Syama Prasad Mookerjee, *Leves from a diary.* Oxford University Pres. New Delhi, 1993, p.40.

48 Tripur Chandra Sen, *op.cit.,*p. 21.

49 *Ibid.,* p. 20.

50 *Tripura District Gazetteers, op.cit.*

taste their fortune. The dreams of the rulers of Tripura to make it a modern one was very much reliant on the fate of those immigrant people. Thus, it becomes necessary to investigate whether the developmental process towards modernisation in Tripura was achieved by the rulers of Tripura with the help of those immigrants.

Chapter IV

Development and the Way to Modernisation

The process of modernization, which was started by the progressive rulers of Tripura, continued in the first two decades of the 20th century. The causes behind immigration remain almost the same as before. The economic push and pull factors that were working in the last quarter of the 19th-century immigration continued.

According to the 1901 Census, 91 per cent of the population depended on agriculture for their livelihood, 3 per cent only on cottage and village industries and handicrafts and the rest on various services and professions. This maximum dependence on agriculture was due to the fact that in the last 20th of the 19th century the rulers of Tripura, to the extent the cultivation and to increase the land revenue encouraged the Bengali cultivators of the neighbouring British districts to immigrate into the State. The *Jangalabadi* system introduced by the rulers of Tripura in the 19th century also encouraged the cultivators of the adjoining territories to immigrate to Tripura.

The rulers of Tripura offered various incentives to the migrants. To attract the cultivators from the adjoining territories of Hill Tipperah the Rajas of Tripura kept the rates of rent very low.

In fact, the rulers of Tripura encouraged the cultivators of the adjoining territories of Tripura mainly for two reasons. Firstly, they wanted to boost up the revenue of the state by giving out land rights to persons settling in

Tripura for farming and to increase the total production of agricultural products. Secondly, the rulers of Tripura were always inspired by the culture and literature of Bengal and therefore, they always tried to sustain a cultural bridge between the people of Bengal and Tripura. Hence, "Tripura was like an *El Dorado* to the hordes of land-hungry people, who almost frenzily grabbed easily culturable fertile valley lands almost in a low prices or by paying a nominal 'najrana' (tribute) to the king".[51] Nevertheless, "none but the most needy amongst the lowest classes of the people can be induced to immigrate into this country".[52]

It is also evident that the Bengali Muslims were much more in number than the Bengali Hindus in Tripura in that period. The rulers of Tripura continued the permanent settlement in Tripura and instead of distributing small pieces of land to the immigrant cultivators, they used to give a vast area of land to the rich and sophisticated persons of Colonial Bengal. The rulers thought that if the rich, educated and resourceful persons took the land then by their endeavour roads and another way of communication also would be built up which would open the way for general advancement and prosperity of the State.

Accordingly, the Census Report of 1901 reveals that the educated people in Tripura were very few in number. The person those who were educated especially belong to the Bengali immigrants. "Till the thirties, the 'thakur' families represented the educated section of the tribals."[53] According to the Imperial Gazetteers of India, Vol. XIII, only 2.3 per cent of the population could read and write and the number of pupils increased to 3125 (3008 boys and 117 girls) in the year 1903-04. The number of educational

---

51   J . B. Ganguly, *Economic Problems Of The Jhumias Of Tripura*, Bookland Private Ltd. Calcutta, 1969, p. 64.

52   Annual Report on the General Administration of the Political Agency of Hill Tippera for the Year 1886 , *op.cit*, para – 29.

53   Hamlet Bareh, *Encyclopedia of North-East India: Vol. VIII, Tripura*, Mittal Publications, Delhi, 2007, p.41.

institutions was 103 in Tripura.[54] Table 4.1 shows the educated aborigines of Tripura in the year 1901.

Table 4.1.

Educational Statement of the census 1901.

Total Population	1, 73,325	
Name of the Tribes	**Population**	**Educated Tribes**
Chakma	4,510	10
Tripura	75,781	107
Kuki	7,547	04
Halam	2,215	Nil
Lushai	135	Nil
Mog	1,491	137
Total	91,679	258

Source: *Census Report 1310 T.E. (1901 A.D.)*, Tribal Research Institute, Government of Tripura, Agartala, Re-print 1995, pp. 17-18.

The table depicts that the educated aborigines were only a few in number for running the administrative machinery of the state. Hence, it became necessary for the progressive rulers of Tripura to invite educated persons to run the administration efficiently and to make it a modern one. Nevertheless, from the census of 1901, it is also clear that the number of educated Hindus in Tripura were much more in number than the educated Muslims.

The process, which was started to attract the educated Bengali people in Tripura by the rulers, continued in the period under review. The Bengali educated people and the members of the Royal family of Tripura occupied all the lucrative posts in Tripura. However, the educated Bengalis began to take maximum interest in the administration of Tripura when an order was published on 1326 T.F. (1916-17A.D.), regarding Tripura State Civil Service.

---

54   *Imperial Gazetteers of India*. op.sit. p. 122.

"The Tripura State Civil Service was renovated on the basis of the order issued by Maharaja Manikya Bahadur on 5th and 15th *Chaitra*, 1326 T.E. and they are as follows:

1. After the declaration of this order nobody will be accepted in the service other then a B.A. degree-holder of the Calcutta University and whose age does not exceed 30 years.

2. The service included the following posts:
   a. Chief Judge of the Khas Court.
   b. Second Judge of the Khas Court.
   c. First Assistant to the Chief Dewan.
   d. Second Assistant to the Chief Dewan.
   e. Private Secretary to the Maharaja Manikya Bahadur.
   f. Assistant Managers of Chakla Roshnabad.
   g. Collectors, Magistrate and Munsiffs.
   h. General Treasury Officer.
   i. Police Superintendent.
   j. Assistant Police Superintendent.
   k. Naib Dewan to *Sanshar* Office.
   l. Settlement Officer.
   m. Assistant Settlement Officer.
   n. Second Officers to the Magistrates of the Divisions
   o. Deputy Sadar Magistrate.
   p. Forest Officer.
   q. Inspector of Schools.
   r. Auditor.
   s. Sub-divisional Officer.
   t. Sub-Manager of Laharpur.
   u. Sub-Manager of Chakla.
   v. Sadar Registrar, Agartala.[55]

---

55 *Tripura State Gazette Sankalan, 1903-1949*, Education Directorate, Government of Tripura, p. 71.

Hence, it becomes clear that the educated Bengalis got an ample opportunity to enter the administrative setup of the State. Not only in the administrative machinery but also in the other welfare departments, the Bengalis made themselves indispensable.

To increase the revenue, it became essential for the rulers of the state to invite those efficient and experienced Bengali administrators. Under the supervision of efficient revenue officers, the tax collection increased rapidly. Also, those efficient revenue officers diversified the source of state revenue. Because of those Bengali educated immigrants, the revenue administration became much more efficient and turned out to be a profit-making agency for the rulers. Table 4.2 clearly shows the enhancement of revenue collection.

Table 4.2.

Collection of Revenues of some specific years.

Years	Revenue
1881-82	2.4 lakhs
1892-93	4.6 lakhs
1901-02	7.06 lakhs
1903-04	8.17 lakhs
1910-11	10.93 lakhs
1911-12	10.4 lakhs
1912-13	11.06 lakhs
1930-31	13.9 lakhs

Source: 1. *Imperial Gazetteers of India.* Vol. XIII, Oxford University Press, London, 1908, p. 121,

2. *Tripura State Gazette Sankalan (1903-1949),* Director of Education, Government of Tripura, November, 1971, p.43,

3. Jalad Baran Ganguly, *An Economic History of North East India, 1826 to 1947,* Akansha Publishing House, New Delhi, 2006, p.449.

Therefore, the educated Bengali immigrants not only made their future bright and established in Tripura but also made the ruler happy by increasing the revenue and by improving their image in the eyes of the British Government.

In the process of modernization, lots of schools including primary and secondary schools were established. In the year 1922(1332 T.E.) the number of schools was one hundred and sixty-eight and among them, six were Primary English schools, and five English High schools. In the next ten years, fifty-six new schools were established and among those new schools, there were six English High schools and two Primary English Schools.[56] A bold step had been taken by the royal administration in 1931-32 when compulsory primary education was introduced in Agartala, under the State Act 2 of 1932 and later it was decided to expand its scope up to the valley of Howrah and to the linked areas of the Sub-divisional town.[57] But before her merger with the Indian union, Tripura had no facilities within her boundary for imparting collegiate education. Table 4.3 depicts the number of primary schools from the year 1907 to 1946.

Table 4.3.

Number of Primary schools in Tripura from 1907 to 1946

Year	Number of Schools	Number of pupils
1907-08	137	4,011
1916-17	125	4,842
1926-27	139	4,215
1936-37	111	5,110
1943-46	123	5,115

Source: *Tripura District Gazetteers*, Government of Tripura, Agartala, 1975, p. 316.

As the number of schools increased during the period, it became necessary to provide a sufficient number of educated teachers to run those schools.

---

56 Takhur Shri Somendra Chandra Devbarma, *op.cit.* p. 62.

57 *Tripura District Gazetteers*, op.cit. p. 316.

However, table 4.4 shows that the educated people in Tripura, from the year 1901 to 1941 were quite a few in number.

Table 4.4.

Literacy in Tripura during 1901 – 1941.

Year	Total % of literates	Male	Female
1901	2.5	4.5	0.2
1911	4.0	6.9	0.8
1921	8.2	14.3	1.1
1931	2.8	4.9	0.4
1941	7.9	12.7	2.5

Source: 1. *Census Report 1310 T.E. (1901 A.D.)*, Tribal Research Institute, Government of Tripura, Agartala, Re-print 1995, p. 16.
2. *Census Bibarani 1340 T.E. (1931 A.D)*, Tribal Research and Cultural Institute, Government of Tripura, Agartala, Re-print 1997, p. 60.
3. Census of India 1961, Vol. XXVI, Tripura, Part I (i), p.296.

Table 4.5.

Number of English educated persons

Year	Number of English Educated persons
1901	324
1911	1208
1921	1707
1931	3087

Source: *Census Bibarani 1340 T.E. (1931 A.D)*, Tribal Research and Cultural Institute, Government of Tripura, Agartala, Re-print 1997, p.61

Table no. 4.5 also depicts that the number of English educated people in Tripura were quite a few but the trends were always upward. However, it is also true that the percentage of literacy as given in table no. 4.4 does not depict the picture of really educated people in Tripura who can truly provide education to others. Thus Thakur Shri Somendra Chandra Devbarma in his *Census Bibarani of Tripura, 1340 T.E.,* opined that "in the census, word educated does not mean highly educated person but the person who can either read or write a letter was considered as educated".[58] Now it is evident from table no. 4.6 that, the numbers of educated people in Bengal were much higher than the number of Tripura.

Table 4.6.

Literacy rate of Tripura and Bengal (1931)

	No. of literates (per thousand)	Male	Female
Tripura	28	49	4
Bengal	110	180	32

Source: *Census Bibarani 1340 T.E. (1931 A.D)*, Tribal Research and Cultural Institute, Government of Tripura, Agartala, Re-print 1997, p. 60.

Hence, the rulers of Tripura through various advertisements invited the candidates from Bengal. If we undergo one of those advertisements of the Government of Tripura it can be understood the role of the rulers of Tripura through those advertisements to induce the graduate unemployed youths of Bengal to join the services of Tripura.

Advertisement

2nd Sravana- 1330 T.E.

Applications are invited for the following posts for H.E. Schools within the State on or before the 15th August,'20 with pay noted against. Apply to the undersigned with testimonials.

S.C.Barman
Officer-in-charge,
EducationDepartment,
Agartala, Tippera State.

---

58   *Ibid.* p. 60.

1. *One B.Sc. on Rs. 50-5-75*

2. *One B.A. strong in English and History Rs. 50-5-75.*

3. *One Normal passed Asst. Teacher with knowledge of Drill & Drawing on Rs. 20.*

4. *One Anglo-Sanskrit teacher holding Govt. title Kabyatirtha qualified upto I.A. or F.A. standard on Rs. 30-2-50.*

5. *One Final Madrassa passed Anglo-Persian teacher qualified upto I.A. or F.A. standard on Rs. 30 rising to 40*

6. *One Final Madrassa passed Maulvi on Rs. 20.*

7. *One B.T. with special training in Geography on Rs.70 p.m.*

8. *One Under-graduate Asst. Teacher on Rs. 30-2-50.*[59]

Advancement in health services was also a part of modernization. The rulers of Tripura though laid their attention in this arena later but it was the difficult communication system in the state and the age-long customs and prejudices as well as the ignorance among the local tribes of Tripura, which became the barrier on the road to progress.[60] The first ruler of Tripura who could realize the use of scientific and modern methods of medical treatment was Maharaja Birchandra Manikya. In the year 1904, the first general hospital named Victoria Memorial Hospital came into existence to commemorate the rule of Queen Victoria. Efficient administrative staff and administrators were appointed in the hospital.[61] The rulers of Tripura patronized all the systems of medical treatment – allopathic, homoeopathic and Ayurveda. But the rulers of Tripura couldn't provide efficient staff and administrators from the indigenous source. Hence, they had to depend on Bengal for those competent and professional medical staff and administrators.

---

59 *Tripura State Gazette Sankalan ,op.cit.,*p. 103.

60 *Tripura District Gazetteers,* Government of Tripura, Agartala, 1975, p.347.

61 Ibid., p. 348.

The rulers of Tripura were so happy with the material progress of Tripura that they did not leave a stone unturned to satisfy the immigrants and how the immigrants are welcomed by the rulers can be noticed from an advertisement which appeared in the Tripura State Gazette in 1916-17.

NOTICE
*(30*th *Agrahayana, 1326 T.E.)*

"All are hereby informed that, recently, in a place, named Kalyanpur, within the jurisdiction of the independent state of Tripura, a new sub-division has been started by the government. For the development of this subdivision, it is essential that people of various castes like washer-men (dhopa), barber (napit), blacksmith (kamar), potter (kumbhakar) etc. should settle there. If any person, belonging to any of these professions, intends to go and settle there permanently along with his family, he will be given land with a minimum of premium and also with appropriate rent-remission. Further, all other amenities necessary for his setting there may also be provided. The local market at Kalyanpur offers good business opportunities. As the various government offices and judicial courts will be there, none need fear of being harassed. A charitable dispensary has also been opened for the benefit of all concerned. No businessmen should miss this opportunity."[62]

The first tea garden of Tripura was *Heeracheera Tea Estate* of Kailashahar Division and was started on 1326 T.E. (1917 A.D.).[63] The tea cultivation was a profit-making enterprise and due to the scarcity of tea cultivation land in Assam and Colonial Bengal, the rich merchants of Bengal began to pay attention towards the moorland of Hill Tipperah and within 14 years from 1917 to 1931 the number of tea gardens increased to 50. In Sadar Division, the numbers of tea estates were 22, in Kailashahar - 18, Khowai - 2, Dharmanagar – 7, Subroom 1 respectively.[64]

---

62   *Tripura State Gazette*, 30th Agrahayana, 1326 T.E.

63   *Census Bibarani 1340 T.E. (1931 A.D)*, op.cit. p. 108

64   Ibid.

It is apparent that the people of the same community did not settle themselves in the same profession. Some communities like, Kanda, Khaira, Pan or Panika, Bhumija, Munda, Lodha, Santal did not settled themselves only in the tea gardens but also in agriculture.

In the initial stage of tea cultivation in Tripura, it was not easy for the tea garden owners to collect the labours for tea cultivation. Tea cultivation is labour intensive. The process of tea cultivation like hoeing, weeding, pruning of the bushes, demands lots of labour and the local tribal and non-tribal people of Tripura did not take interest to work in the plantation due to the low wages and peculiar nature of the tea plantation industry.[65] Therefore, the owners of the farms had to depend on the labours of states like Bihar, Orissa, Madhya Pradesh and United Provinces.

Accordingly, the Royal Government of Tripura also took a keen interest in providing labour for those tea gardens and the steps taken in this concern were found in some of the letters written to the Political Agent of Tripura by the Minister of Tripura State.

Letter to the Political Agent of Tripura by Minister of Tripura State on 6th June 1921

"I am directed by the Durbar to address you in a matter of great importance in connection with the trouble due to the exodus of coolies from the Assam Tea Gardens, the alleged incidents at Chandpur and the unfortunate strikes and hartals all over the country which have affected this territory along with the bordering British Districts. You have already been informed by me, and His Highness's Chief Secretary and Private Secretary of the recent troubles into which the Durbar have been dragged by the agitators.

2. This situation has given rise to a thought in his Highness's mind as to how he could render some services to the Imperial Government in the

---

65 P. N .Bhattacherjee &Ram Gopal Singh, *Tea Plantation and the Tribes of Tripura*, Tripura State Tribal Cultural Research Institute and Museum, Govt. of Tripura, Agartala, 1995, p.40.

midst of this general turmoil. A solution presents itself of His Highness in offering a decent livelihood to the disaffected coolies in this territory. The Durbar are prepared to find shelter, land and employment for them if they choose to come and settle in this territory. They are ready to receive all the coolies (with the exception of those who are lying ill) stranded at Chandpur, pay for Railway fare of Akhaura if the Assam-Bengal Railway demands the same and give them food and shelter on the following understanding among other things which may be settled in conference with the coolies, their advisers, popular leaders and the Government of Bengal:

i. *If the coolies agree to settle in this territory the Durbar will grant some land to each family for cultivation and building their houses on. No rent shall be payable for such lands for the first year of settlement – a reasonable rent shall be assessed on the expiry of the year and this rent will be regulated from time to time by the laws of the land governing the relationship of landlord and tenant.*

ii. *The Durbar will supply temporary cottage for the immediate shelter of the coolies and feed them for 3 days of their arrival.*

iii. *The Durbar will be ready to receive batches of 508 souls dayly, 3 days after their intention to come here is intimated to the Durbar.*

iv. *The A. B. Railway should undertake to carry the coolies at Chandpur free of fare or at reduced fare or even at full fare to be paid by the Durbar in the event of their refusal to grant concessions.*

v. *The Durbar will not receive the persons who are lying ill at Chandpur and their families until they are all right and declared fit to travel. State doctors will examine and pass them before they are taken charge of at Chandpur.*

vi. *The coolies will be free to serve anybody they like. If it is desired, the Durbar will themselves employ them if they want.*

vii. *A census of the coolies will be taken by the State Agents before they depart from Chandpur.*

viii. *No one will be forced to live a life of labour if he wants to turn a cultivator.*

ix. *The Durbar shall provide Civil protection, Medical aid and the education for the coolies at their settlement.*

x. *The coolies shall be free to leave their territory at anytime they like or should they desire to go back to their ancestral homes or change their residence.*

3. The Durbar will feel thankful by your kind intervention in obtaining the approval of the Government of Bengal to these proposals by immediate. Telegraphic communication as there is no time to loose and request you to be so good as to place yourself in communication with the local Government Officers, popular leaders.

From those letters, it became clear that how the rulers of Tripura eagerly wanted those labourers to immigrate into the state so that a solution can be made regarding the scarcity of workers in the tea gardens of Tripura. The administration of Tripura also shows their intense desire to provide various facilities for those immigrants labourers.

Those labour immigrants permanently settled themselves in Tripura. However, due to economic depression in the world, the production of tea decreased, as shown in table 4.7, but it was evident that the number of tea garden labours in Tripura increased.

Table 4.7.

Production of Tea in Tripura (1923 to 1931).

Year	In Pound
1923	2,25,533
1924	3,38,272
1925	5,60,568

Continued…

1926	8,20,615
1927	9,40,062
1928	10,57,408
1929	14,02,725
1930	12,49,374

Source: *Census Bibarani 1340 T.E. (1931 A.D)*, Tribal Research and Cultural Institute, Government of Tripura, Agartala, Re-print 1997, p.109

The Chakmas are basically *Jhum* cultivators and thus they moved from palace to place in search of *Jhum* lands and in the course of that they entered Tripura and settled down there permanently because Tripura provided them sufficient scope of *Jhum* lands. This is evident from a survey report on a village named Dwarika Talukdar Para, which was mentioned by J. B. Ganguli in his book 'The Benign Hill'. In the survey, report it was stated that "The village first came to be inhabited by four Chakma families headed by a Chakma leader, Dwarika Talukdar, in 1927. They were followed by Mogs, Muslims and Tripuris in 1940, 1945 and 1951 respectively. The Chakmas came here from the adjoining Chittagong Hill Tracts because of growing population pressure and non-availability of cultivable land."[66]

Table no. 4.8 shows that while Jhum cultivation was the predominant form of economic activities among the Chakmas, a good number of Mogs took to plough cultivation as the main occupation retaining Jhum cultivation a subsidiary occupation.

---

66   J.B.Ganguli, *The Benign Hills, op.sit.*, p. 31.

Table 4.8.

Practice of cultivation among Chakma and Mog in 1931.

Tribe	Total Population	Shifting Cultivation	Plough cultivation	Other activities
Chakma	8,730	1407	57	35
Mog	5,748	885	523	194

Source: *Census Bibarani 1340 T.E.* (1931 A.D), Tribal Research and Cultural Institute, Government of Tripura, Agartala, Re-print 1997. pp.170-171

Though it is not evident from the sources that whether the increase in the number of Manipuris was due to their migration or not, but it was true that the Manipuris were true agriculturalists and according to the Census Bibarani 1340 T.E., in the year 1931, 4,171 Manipuri people took plough cultivation as their main occupation and 2,641 people as their subsidiary occupation.[67] Thus, though the political disorder as mentioned earlier was the cause of Manipuri migration in Tripura, occurred in the last part of the 19th century but the economic pull factor may be the other cause of Manipuri migration in the period under review. The *Jangalabadi* system introduced by the ruler of Tripura encouraged the Manipuris to settle in Tripura. In *Tripura Rajye Tirish Bochor* (Thirty Years in Tripura), *Dharmanagar Division*, Brjendra Chandra Dutta reveals that many Manipuris have taken up land under the *Jangalabadi* system for farming purposes. Usually, they choose to live near the forests and therefore after recovering some forest land for the agricultural purpose they sell the plots to the immigrants Bengali cultivators and shift to lands still closer to the forests.[68]

The Khasis immigrated to Tripura after 1931 and they were basically betel leaf cultivators in Tripura. They are the good cultivator of *Pan* (betel leaf)

---

67 Ibid. p. 171.

68 Brjendra Chandra Dutta, *Tripura Rajye Tirish Bochor* (Thirty Years in Tripura), *Dharmanagar Division*, (In Bengali), Education Directorate, Government of Tripura, Agartala, 1972, p. 11.

and were heartily accepted by the Royal court. They settled themselves in the Kulaihaor area.[69] Based on the Consolidated Administration Report of the Tripura State for 1347, 1348 and 1349 T.E., B. P. Misra opined that in 1943 the cultivation of *Pan* by the Khasias in Dalucherra block had made very good progress. The commodity was sold in Kamalpur, Halhali and Chhellengma bazaar and it is gratifying to note that the production was more than sufficient to meet the local requirement, the surplus being exported to the adjoining British districts.[70]

The rulers of Tripura tried their best to improve the economic condition of their state and for improvement; they gave much more impetus to settled cultivation. As mentioned earlier, for settled cultivation they invited the Bengal cultivators in the State. For settled cultivation, the plains land adjoining to British districts were first taken up for renovation. The cultivators from Colonial Bengal were invited to utilize the plains land of Tripura instead of rent to be paid to the ruler of Tripura. Those tenants were known as "Ziratia". The *Ziratia* were subjects of British India but owned land within the independent state of Hill Tipperah.[71] They were a distinctive group of non-resident tenants. They migrated to the host country for various reasons but they move on economic grounds. "Ziratia" peasants are the temporary migrants in Tripura.

Ziratia peasants were the special kind of farmers who used to migrate temporarily into Tripura during the agricultural season. They used to migrate into the state at their own convenience. In the state, they used to construct temporary huts of their own and cultivate certain plots of land and produce crops thereon.[72] When they completed the whole process of harvesting, they used to go back to their own homes in Colonial India. Nevertheless, before they went back to their home they had to pay rent to the rulers of Tripura in form of "either cash or in-kind" as it was settled

---

69   Bani Prasanna Misra, *op.cit*, p. 19.

70   *Ibid.*

71   *Ibid.* p.22

72   Tripur Chandra Sen, *Tripura In Transition (1923-1957)*, Agartala, Tripura, 1970, p.89.

at the time of their agreement. "On rare occasions when Tripura faced food shortage the state-imposed restrictions on the *Ziratia* tenants to take out of the state paddy in excess of what was actually needed to meet the consumption requirements of their families."[73] The *Ziratia* peasants were basically Bengali Muslims of the neighbouring districts[74] of British India, especially from Tipperah, Noakhali and Sylhet. As said by Nagendra Jamatia, ex-MLA of Tripura, "During the period of World War II, there was the scarcity of labour in Tripura and to fulfill the demands of *Zamindari* the people, both Hindus and Muslims, were collected from the border lands of Chakla Roshnabad on the basis of *Ziratia* system…. The numbers of those Ziratia peasants were approximately 80,000."[75]

However, the pull factors were not only the root cause of migration in Tripura but the economic push factors were similarly responsible for the migration under review. In the early 20th century colonial India was facing the adverse effect of unemployment in the Government services. Schools, colleges, govt. offices were established in different parts of the country but there were no sufficient jobs to fulfil the occupational requirements of the unemployed youths. In addition, the attitude of the British Government provoked them to take all the lucrative jobs and administrative official posts. Accordingly, Tripura became an easy target for those job-hungry educated Bengalis. As observed by J B Ganguli that during the period, Colonial India was facing much economic hardship in comparison to the conditions of Tripura. The state provided secured employment with higher real wages (money wage was low but the price level was even lower) and a number of free bonuses were offered. He also observed that in Tripura, education for the children was free and a college functioning in the state

---

73 Jalad Baran Ganguly, *An Economic History of North East India, 1826 to 1947,* Akansha Publishing House, New Delhi, 2006, p.426.

74 Bani Prasanna Misra, *op.cit,* p.22.

75 Nagendra Jamatia, Ex- MLA, Tripura State Legislative Assembly, Interview taken on 1st June 2010, Tuesday, at 4.00 p.m.

provided employment opportunities for the college teachers from outside who were in search of jobs.[76]

It is evident that the people who depended on agriculture generally never shift themselves from their own land unless they are pressurized politically, mistreated economically and socially, or victimized by natural calamities. The agriculturalists of the adjoining districts of Tripura who migrated from their lands to Hill Tipperah in the late 19th century were victimized by the political and economic policy of the Colonial Government in Bengal. The question thus arises, why then the cultivators of the Colonial Bengal left their own lands and took shelter in the hilly regions of Tripura. In fact, the political and economic causes were the major factors.

The Permanent Settlement was not at all suitable for the peasants of Bengal. The revenue was so high that it became impossible for the poor peasants to pay. Along with it, the peasants had to face the ruthless attitude of the *Zamindars*. The survival of the peasants became unbearable. To fulfil the demands of the British Government and to save their landlords the *Zamindars* had to pay their revenues in time. Thus they made each and every effort to collect the revenue in due course and if possible much more from the poor peasants. The draught, the famine or any other natural calamities never stopped the *Zamindars* to collect revenue from the peasants. Thus the peasants often began to depend on the moneylenders to pay the revenue or sometimes they became the day labourers in the house of the *Zamindars*. Consequently, the conditions of the cultivators were not pleasing under the revenue settlement of Colonial Bengal. Also in the *Rayatwari* areas, the cultivators were directly tyrannized by the revenue-hungry British Government. The rent was high and the peasants suffered a lot in the hands of the Government if they failed to pay the revenue in time. Many contemporary European writers after noticing the above situation reveal the conditions of the peasants in their writing. In 1826, Bishop Heber observes, "Neither native nor European agriculturalist, I think, can thrive at the present rate of taxation. Half of the gross produce

---

76   J.B.Ganguli, *The Benign Hills, op.sit.*, p. 12.

of the soil in a general feeling among the King's officers …. That the peasantry in the Company's Provinces are on the whole worse off, poorer and more dispirited than the subjects of the Native Prince …. The fact is, no Native Prince demands the rest which we do."[77] In Bengal, the relations between the '*Zamindars*' and the tenants were basically governed by the Bengal Tenancy Act of 1885, which secured the status and privileges of all classes of tenants. However, the Act was modified by Bengal Act I of 1907 "with the object of giving greater facilities to landlords for the collection of rent…"[78] This Act was in force in all the Eastern Bengal districts, except the Chittagong Hill Tracts. As regards Eastern Bengal, the Act was amended in 1908 but following the same lines as the Bengal Act of 1907. Though the "main provisions are now, fairly well known both to landlords and to tenants; but there are indications that the importance of various sections has not yet been realized by the public. The levy of *abwabs* or illegal cesses in addition to rent continues to prevail more or less throughout the Presidency. It is reported that, as a rule, the tenants pay these illegal demands without much demur to escape harassment in other ways."[79]

Thus the economic suppression made by the *Zamindars*, moneylenders and the British Government to the poor peasants of the adjacent districts of Hill Tipperah, compelled them to migrate into the hilly region of Tripura for their livelihood.

The density of population in the adjoining Bengal districts of Hill Tipperah may be the other root cause of migration. The neighbouring districts of Colonial Bengal like Tipperah (Comilla), Sylhet, Noakhali, and the Chittagong Hill Tracts were overpopulated during the period and that huge population created pressure on the cultivable lands of those territories. Thus, due to that overburden on the land, the people were bound to leave their place of birth and search for a better living place and Hill Tipperah became an easy target for those land-hungry people. The growth rates of

---

77 J. B. Ganguli, *The Benign Hills, op.sit.*, p. 21.

78 S. C. Ray, *Land Revenue Administration in India*, Calcutta University, 1915, p.20.

79 Ibid.

the population of those areas were much more than the growth rate of the whole of Bengal. While in Bengal the average of cultivated areas per family of agriculturists in 1931 was 4.84 acres, it was 2.99 for Tipperah, 3.33 for Noakhali and 3.47 acres of Chittagong.[80]

Thus, it has been observed that both the push and pull factors were responsible for those migrations. The rulers of Tripura to modernize their states pulled the educated intelligentsia of Bengal as well as the plough cultivators of Bengal. The rulers of Tripura provided all sorts of facilities to those immigrants of Bengal. Those migrants were solely economic migrants. The period not only witnessed the flow of Bengali immigrants but various others tribes like *Chakmas, Mogs, Santals, Orangs, Bhils, Mundas, Khasis, Panika* etc. from various parts of British India. The establishment of Tea gardens in Tripura during this period was also a stimulus for the immigrant Tribal communities. They were also economic migrants.

In the 1st half of the 20th century Tripura also witnessed a major change in the political scenario of Colonial India. The nationalist movements, communal turmoil in India and the changed socio-economic circumstances of Colonial Bengal pushed the Bengalis of the adjoining territories of Bengal towards Tripura. Tripura thus witnessed not the economic migrants but also the political and ethnic migrants in the form of displaced persons and refugees. During those years, a princely state like Hill Tipperah also viewed the temporary migrants like the *Ziratia* peasants and the "revolutionary activists" of British India.

Therefore, due to the flow of the huge number of migrants from the year 1901 to 1947, in various forms, there came a huge change in the social and economic structure of the princely state Tripura. Now whether those social and economic structural changes can be considered as development for the state of Tripura is a matter of investigation and analysis. Hence, there needs an elaborate assessment considering the socio-economic changes in Tripura during the period of our study.

---

80 Hamlet Bareh, *Encyclopedia of North-East India: Vol. VIII, Tripura*, Mittal Publications, Delhi, 2007, p.14.

Chapter V

Socio-Economic Development

The fundamental base of the society of Tripura was its tribal culture and beliefs. The cultural sphere of Tripura involves an extensive range of multi-dimensional features. Tripura always preserved multiple cultures of her own and the social structure of Tripura demonstrates a harmonious co-existence of various tribal and non-tribal communities. Thus, one finds elements of culture, of different sets of people, each unique in its own way mingled together, and in the process, a composite culture is embracing the different strands of faith.

Tripura was a princely state, ruled by the famous Manikya rulers and the period from 1900 to 1947 was the last half of the Manikya dynasty. The pressure on the society due to migration continued during the period of Regency (1947 –1949).

Hence, the society of hill Tripura was certainly going to have an impact on the society. In essence, migration had some implications in the modernization drive of the society of Tripura. It is an acknowledged fact that when a society experiences modernization, it confronts new culture and values. However, in the society of Tripura, diverse tribal culture embedded for centuries, but the unrestricted inflows of migrants have led to the occurrence of gradual cultural transformation in Tripura.

Hence, it becomes necessary to highlight the composition of the tribal and non-tribal population of the society in Tripura. This is intending to examine the cultural intermixture and value dynamics.

Table 5.1.

Composition of Tribal and Non-tribal Population in Tripura (1901 to1941)

Year	Total Population	Tribal Population	Non-Tribal Population	Tribal growth (%)	Non-Tribal growth (%)
1901	1,73,325	91,679	81,646	-	-
1911	2,29,613	1,11,303	1,18,310	21.41	44.91
1921	3,04,437	1,71,610	1,32827	54.18	12.27
1931	3,82,450	2,03,327	1,79,123	18.48	34.85
1941	5,13,010	2,56,991	2,56,019	26.39	42.93

Source: 1. Atish Chandra Choudhury, Census Report 1310 T.E. (1901 A.D.), Tribal Research Institute, Government of Tripura, Agartala, Re-printing 1995, p. 18.

2. S.R. Bhattacharjee, *Tribal Insurgency in Tripura: A Study in Exploration of Causes,* Inter-India Publications, New Delhi, 1989, p. 39.

It becomes clear from table no. 5.1 that the massive increase of non-tribal population in the state during that period equalled the number of the aborigines of the state. At the end of the monarchical regime in the state of Tripura, she was converted from a tribal hilly state to a non-tribal one. It was only due to the flow of immigrants in Tripura, especially the Bengalis. Society is always led by the majority but it is the dynamic part of the society that after the majorities' rule it always tries to maintain equilibrium between the majority and the other minority groups. It is evident from the table (No. 5.1) that during the period under study, the non-Tribal population was dominant in the Tribal state like Tripura.

In Tripura, the non-tribal population headed by the Bengalis was patronized by the Royal court of Tripura. The tribal rulers of Tripura always gave importance to Bengali culture. They were very much acquainted with the culture and literature of Bengal. The main fabric of the society of Tripura is an active reflection of a certain image, and that image is nothing but the respect for the language and culture of Bengal. Later the respect and admiration for the Bengali culture and language, have taken roots among the aborigines of Tripura, which influenced different aspects of the society of Tripura like her education, health, dress, food habits, social administration, marriage and customary life of the aborigines.

Modern educated Bengali immigrants influenced the educational system of Tripura. The literacy growth rates of Tripura from the year 1901 to 1941 was not very impressive in contrast to the number of increased immigrants. It was due to the illiteracy of the local tribal people as well as the immigrant Bengali agriculturalists.

The educated migrants increased the literacy growth rate of the state. Moreover, it paved the way to increase the number of educational institutions in the state (Table No.5.2).

Table 5.2.

Number of Institutions (Primary, Basis and non-Basic) and pupils.

Year	Number of Schools	Number of pupils
1907-08	137	4,011
1916-17	125	4,842
1926-27	139	4,215
1936-37	111	5,110
1943-46	123	5,115

Source: 1. *Tripura District Gazetteers*, Government of Tripura, Agartala, 1975, p. 322.

Women's education got its impetus. In the 1st half of the 20th century i.e. before the amalgamation, there was only 5 lower Primary, 6 Middle and one High English School for girls in Tripura and in the year 1946, only 1,026 nos. of girl students enrolled themselves in the schools. However, as the number of Bengali immigrants began to increase in Tripura after the partition of India, the girl's enrolment began to increase.

Before amalgamation, the Hindu Bengalis, those who immigrated to Tripura were engaged in white-collar jobs and business and thus concentrated in the urban areas. The Muslim Bengali immigrants, on the other hand, were poor, uneducated and thus concentrated themselves in the field of agriculture i.e. in the rural areas. Hence, according to the Census Bibarani, 1931, in the urban area (only the town Agartala) 86% of the people were Hindus and 14% of the people were Muslims.[81]

The rulers of Tripura for their own interests invited the educated Bengali immigrants to modernize the socio-economic and administrative structure of the State. However, this, in turn, became a nightmare to the tribal aborigines of the state and they began to lose their status in their own state. The aborigines of the state Tripura suffered a lot due to immigration.

The Bengali educated people with their advanced educational and scientific knowledge dominated the socio-economic structure of the state as a whole and on the tribal peoples of Tripura in particular. They got maximum opportunities in Government jobs; they have access to mobility and control the economy of the state. On the other hand, due to the lack of proper education and modern skill, the aborigines of the state lost their social mobility. The Bengali people considered those uneducated, poor and rural tribal aborigines as uncultured.

Nevertheless, this is one side of the impact of migration, which was probably the darkest one. The other side was just its opposite, where due to close interaction between the two diverse cultures and traditions, a new composite culture emerged in Tripura. This composite culture was the synthesis of the Bengali immigrants and the aborigines of Tripura. Hence, Tripura was termed as, "a laboratory of exotic cultural synthesis".[82]

---

81 Takhur Shri Somendra Chandra Devbarma , *Census Bibarani* (Bengali), Tribal Research and Cultural Institute, Government of Tripura, Agartala, 1997, p.41.

82 Gurmeet Kanwal, V.K. Shrivastava, *Defenders of the dawn: a panorama of Eastern Command*, Lancer Publisher, New Delhi, 2000, p.69.

Because of extremely close contact between the Bengali migrants and the different tribes of Tripura, the Bengali migrants were easily absorbed in the mainstream of society. The migrants now began to flow into the mainstream of socio-cultural activities of Tripura. The Bengali immigrants of this state generally belong to the various districts of East Pakistan. Thus, those Bengali immigrants brought with them the culture of their own districts. With those immigrants, various cultural rites, rituals, ceremonies and festivals entered into the cultural life of the tribal peoples.

Due to the long period of co-existence, the association between the tribals and the Bengalis became much cordial and equally receptive to each other's needs. Matrimonial relations developed between the two communities, along with it the Works of fine art, music and dance manifest the mutual interaction of the two cultural forces. The tribals of the remote areas are much more ethnocentric and they were reluctant to sustain their traditional ethos viz. their dress, ornaments, artefacts, food habit, performance, dance, folksongs and observance of festivities etc. However, their ethnocentrism and reluctance could not save them from the grasp of immigrant culture.

The changes are not found only in the dresses but in the ornaments and the customary lifestyles. The immigrant communities directly or indirectly affected almost all the tribes of Tripura. The food habits of the tribal population in Tripura were also affected by the food habits of those immigrant Bengalis. However, after the influx of Bengali immigrants, they came near the world of spice. The spicy foods of Bengali attracted them and began to put them away from their traditional foods.

Another most important impact of migration was the spread of *Rabindra culture* in Tripura. The rulers of Tripura had a close personal relationship with Rabindranath Tagore. Rabindranath Tagore was attracted by the beauty of Tripura and visited Tripura, seven times. He was in close touch with four successive rulers of Tripura viz. Birchandra Kishore Manikya Bahadur, Radhakishor Manikya Bahadur, Birendra Kishore Manikya Bahadur and King Bir Bikram Kishore Manikya Bahadur. Several times, he received financial assistance from the rulers of Tripura. The unique bondage of love and affection between the rulers of Tripura and Rabindranath Tagore created an environment of *Rabindra culture* in Tripura. Accordingly, the rulers prepared the plot of *Rabindra culture* in Tripura and the Bengali immigrants built the structure on that plot. Rabindranath became an inspiration for both the tribal and non-tribal people of Tripura.

This new path of philosophy attracted the educated tribes of Tripura. They began to think about the world differently. The tribes of Tripura began to be attracted to Bengali literature.

Accordingly, the process of modernisation started by the rulers of Tripura was in progress but the Bengali community, of whom a huge number were the migrants, headed that route of modernisation. However, the impact of migration cannot be measured only from a social perspective. Because the social configuration of a state is to a great extent interlinked with the economic structure of a state.

Tripura had a stagnant, semi-feudal and subsistence economy. She had a very little population with no economic ambitions and thus she was free from economic hassles and anxieties. She never experienced the suffocation of economic insufficiency. There was neither the pressure of population on land nor the pressure of unemployment on the social structure and economic potential. Highlighting the material condition of the people of Hill Tipperah, W.W. Hunter opined, "The hill people, as a rule, are very poor and improvident. A good season means with them merely plenty of pigs to eat and plenty of spirits to drink; a bad season is a next door to starvation. It is difficult to estimate the cost of living among them, as they grow their own food, and breed their own pigs and fowls, and bring away their cotton to market to pay the tax. The fowls are almost invariably offered up in sacrifice before being eaten."[83]

According to Boundary Commissioner's Return, dated March 1875, the total area of Hill Tipperah was approximately 3,867 square miles or

---

83   W.W.Hunter, A Statistical Account of Bengal, Vol. VI, London, 1876, p. 499. (1973 Reprint).

2,474,880 acres and there was no revenue survey of the state from which the cultivated, cultivable but uncultivated and uncultivable and wastelands are shown separately; but there is no doubt that the portion under cultivation forms a very small proportion of the total area.[84]

The people of Tripura depended on agriculture, especially on the Jhuming cultivation. In the past, Tribal people produced everything they consumed. Production included cultivation of crops, collection of forest products, production of textiles, weaving of baskets, making other crafts, fishing and hunting.[85] They did not produce for exchange but for consumption only except cotton and sesamum, which were generally produced to export. "Writing in 1869, Lewin, the then Deputy Commissioner of Chittagong Hill Tracts, had shown that a Jhumia family could comfortably meet their needs from its Jhum and have enough surplus left over for festival and puja expenses, sickness, ornaments and clothes. He estimated that a man and his wife could Jhum 9 kanies (3.6 acres) of land every year."[86] Other than agriculture, the aborigines of the state depended on fishing, hunting and collection of vegetables as a part of their food-gathering activity.

The economic structure of the princely state can be compared with the primitive age culture where people were busy with their hunting, food-gathering and so on. There was no sign of modern socio-economic activities. Hence, it is clear that the rulers of Tripura were not in a state to consider themselves as the rulers of the modern age. Thus, they took the initiative to modernize their state and immigration of Bengalis from Bengal as well as other communities were just a part of that modernisation process,

However, the princely state of Tripura entered the century with a deplorable state of the economy, which is depicted in table no. 5.3.

---

84 Ibid , p. 502
85 J B, Ganguly, *Economic Problems of the Jhumias of Tripura*, Bookland Private Ltd., Calcutta, 1969,13 p. 37.
86 Omesh Saigal, *Tripura: its History and Culture*, Concept Publishing Company, Dehli, 1978, p. 42.

Table 5.3.
Distribution of population (1901 A.D.) based on chief occupation, (including the family members).

	Occupation	Total	Family
1	Royal Service (including all sorts of work)	699	501
2	Proprietor of land	631	2,103
3	Cultivator of his own land	30,102	44,797
4	Agricultural labourer	411	151
5	Jhumia peasants	46,027*	34,248
6	Domestic servants	703	685
7	Hotel owner	6	1
8	Sweeper	53	29
9	Milk, Gee and Fish seller	259	120
10	Bread maker, *Dalwala*, Sweet maker, *Kolu*	321	219
11	Pan, Beetle nut, spice, tobacco, country wine seller	209	92
12	Wood seller	191	229
13	Weaver	2,338	104
14	Iron tools maker	121	13
15	Potter	77	46
16	Tailors	32	1
17	Wood and bamboo traders	112	89
18	Shoe maker	63	104
19	Priest	283	284
20	Medicine seller	81	66
21	Common labour	1,054	723
22	Prostitute	5	1
23	Beggar	509	194

* Among those Jhumia peasants, 9,260 numbers of peasants also follow the plough cultivation.

Source: Atish Chandra Choudhury, *Census Report 1310 T.E. (1901 A.D.)*, Tribal Research Institute, Government of Tripura, Agartala, Re-print 1995, pp. 19-20.

Tripura was totally an agricultural society and was based on Jhum cultivation. Hence, it is obvious that the rulers of Tripura had to depend on the revenue from Chakla Roshnabad for their earnings.

However, in the process of transformation in the first half of the 20th century in Tripura, when the Bengali elites and the Bengali peasants began to immigrate into the state, the revenue collection of the state Tripura began to increase. The educated Bengali peoples like Rai Umakanta Das Bahadur, Babu Nilmani Das, Rai Bahadur Mohini Mohan Bardhan, Ishan Chandra Gupta and others had both the knowledge and experience of administration especially in the field of economy. Hence, by utilizing their talents and experiences, the rulers of Tripura increased the revenue of the state. Since the 19th century while the royal treasury was totally dependent on the revenue of Chakla Roshnabad, shifted the dependency from Chakla Roshnabad to the state Tripura. Table No. 5.4 depicts the clear pictures of the above statement.

Table 5.4.

Gross Revenue from the State proper and Chakla Roshnabad of some specific years in Tripura (in Rs.):

Year	Revenue of Tripura State	Revenue of Chakla Roshnabad
1873-74	1,63,350	n.a.
1874-75	1,86,930	5,14,070
1903-04	8,16,958	8,58,581
1904-05	7,68,206	9,03,906
1913-14	10,36,123	10,21,429
1923-24	15,82,035	11,00,400
1933-34	13,39,810	9,82,889
1943-44	32,60,208	17,63,259

Source: Bani Prasanna Misra, *Socioeconomic Adjustments of Tribals: Case-Study of Tripura Jhumias,* People's Publishing House, New Delhi, 1976, p. 59.

The Bengali illiterate immigrants those who immigrated into Tripura during the period under study were purely agriculturalists and were experts in plough cultivation and hence, they reclaimed more and more lands (Table No. 5.5), which were unexploited and felt aside by the aborigines of the state. The Manipuri people were also good in settled cultivation and thus, they help to reclaim more land in Tripura.

Table 5.5.

Area under cultivation (in hectare)

Year	Area under cultivation
1929-30	164982.24*
1930-31	165500.24*
1937-38	124979.00

** In the source it is given in square miles. But to co-relate it and for better comparison it is converted into hectare.*

Source: 1. Ranjit Kumar Dey, *The Statistical Account of Tripura,* Uppal Publishing House, New Delhi, 2000, p. 27.
2. Tripura District Gazetteers, Education Publications, Department of Education, Government of Tripura, Agartala, 1975, p. 160

The improvement in the number of plough cultivators ultimately upsurges the land revenue of the state in the first half of the 20th century and table no. 5.6 and 5.7 exhibits it. It is evident from those tables that while the percentage of land revenue of the state increased enormously, the percentage of revenue on export duties on cotton, oilseeds and royalties on elephants caught were decreased in the last part of the Manikya rule. It was because the elephants in the forests were becoming scarce due to the frequent movement of the people and the worldwide economic depression (1929-33) had a great impact on the export of cotton. Nevertheless, it is also interesting that the percentage of house tax collected from the Jhumias were also reduced largely during this period. Hence, it became clear that the immigrants had a great impact on the revenue economy of the state. The age-old tradition of Jhum cultivation began to lose its importance in the state economy, and in return, plough or settled cultivation took its place.

Table 5.6.

State Revenue of Tripura – Source wise for the selected year (in thousand rupees)

Year	Land revenue	Tolls on forest produce exported	Export duties on cotton & oilseeds	Royalties on elephant caught	House tax from jhumias	All other sources	Total
1873-74	38.65	27.33	45.69	18.02	24.67	8.99	163.35
1874-75	38.78	40.40	47.18	24.00	24.22	12.35	186.93
1893-94	78.10	151.65	79.18	42.23	40.35	75.50	467.01
1894-95	88.75	157.22	114.36	23.47	37.13	80.20	501.13
1913-14	359.73	307.74	94.88	2.32	45.50	225.95	1036.12
1914-15	342.19	340.98	89.25	-	40.47	222.57	1035.46
1933-34	450.71	347.93	106.84	2.62	46.96	384.75	1339.81
1934-35	644.45	330.06	134.22	2.32	52.59	414.97	1579.61

Source: Bani Prasanna Misra, *Socioeconomic Adjustments of Tribals: Case-Study of Tripura Jhumias,* People's Publishing House, New Delhi, 1976, p.60.

Table 5.7.

Percentage earning under different heads or revenue for the state of Tripura

Year	Land revenue	Tolls on forest produce exported	Export duties on cotton & oilseeds	Royalties on elephant caught	House tax from jhumias	All other sources	Total
1873-74	23.66	16.73	27.97	11.03	14.10	5.50	100.00
1874-75	20.75	21.61	24.24	12.84	12.96	6.61	100.00
1893-94	16.72	32.47	16.95	9.04	8.64	16.17	100.00
1894-95	17.71	31.38	22.82	4.68	7.41	16.00	100.00
1901-02	22.18	21.33	9.8	6.3	4.06	N.A.	100.00
1903-04	23.2	NA	NA	NA	NA	NA	NA
1910-11	32.07	30.9	20.18	7.6	4.8	NA	100.00
1911-12	33.2	NA	NA	NA	NA	NA	NA
1912-13	34.22	NA	NA	NA	NA	NA	NA
1913-14	34.72	29.70	9.16	-	4.39	21.89	100.00
1914-15	33.05	32.93	8.62	-	3.31	21.49	100.00
1930-31	44.01	36.0	10.72	4.1	37.2		100.00
1933-34	33.64	25.97	7.97	-	3.50	28.72	100.00
1934-35	40.80	20.90	8.56	-	3.33	26.27	100.00

Source: 1. Bani Prasanna Misra, *Socioeconomic Adjustments of Tribals: Case-Study of Tripura Jhumias,* People's Publishing House, New Delhi, 1976, p.60.

2. Dipannita Chakraborty, *Land Question in Tripura,* Akansha Publishing House, New Delhi, 2004, p. 44.

3. Jalad Baran Ganguly, *An Economic History of North East India 1826 to 1947*, Akansha Publishing House, New Delhi, 2006, p. 449.

Nevertheless, settled cultivation did not have a uniform growth in each part of the state and it was because the immigrant cultivators did not settle them uniformly, as they entered Tripura from different districts of East Bengal. Coming from various districts of East Bengal like Sylhet, Comilla, Noakhali, Mymensingh, and Chittagong, in Tripura, the immigrants settled themselves in the adjoining territories of Bengal's border (Table No. 5.8). This created a spatial distribution of Bengali immigrant cultivators, which ultimately reflected the regional imbalances to the extent of immigration-induced agricultural development of Tripura.

Table 5.8.

Number of Jhumias, cultivators and agricultural labourers in the various divisions of Tripura (According to Census Report 1931 A.D.)

Division	Jhumias	Cultivators	Agricultural labourers
Sadar	2,172	14,391	1,778
Kailashahar	3,992	7,006	910
Khowai	4,250	4,212	668
Dharmanagar	904	6,522	674
Sonamura	463	4,573	815
Udaipur	1,375	6,011	680
Amarpur	3,119	779	180
Belonia	786	1,968	241
Sabroom	1,002	1,456	265
Total*	18,876	49,514	7,190

* Including the numbers of Buddhists and Christians.

Source: Takhur Shri Somendra Chandra Devbarma, *Census Bibarani* (Bengali), 1340 T.E., Tribal Research and Cultural Institute, Government of Tripura, Agartala, p. 100.

Hence, it is clear from table no. 4.8 that Sadar, Kailashahar, Dharmanagar, Udaipur and Sonamura divisions were dominated by the plough cultivators while Khowai and Amarpur were dominated by the Jhumias and that distribution played a leading role in framing the economy of that particular division.

The trends of settled cultivation or plough cultivation were exaggerated in the first half of the 20th century, due to the immigrants and especially the Bengali immigrants. During the period the number of agricultural labourers also increased significantly. Table no. 5.9 depicts the trend of cultivators and agricultural labourers in Tripura from the year 1901 to 1951.

Table 5.9.

Trend of cultivators and agricultural labourers in Tripura from the year 1901 to 1951 (in %)

Year	Cultivators	Agricultural labourers
1901	35.71	0.49
1931	56.79	10.29
1951	62.94	8.93

Source: Compiled from various Census reports.

From the table, it becomes clear that in each consecutive decade the number of cultivators and agricultural labourers increased in Tripura, which, eventually boost up the state economy with increased crop production.

The growth rates of some specific crops help us to comprehend the nature of migrants, their methods of cultivation and the agricultural economy of the state.

Table 5.10.

Production of Main Crops of some specific years in Metric tons.

Year	Production in '000 M.T.*					
	Rice	Jute	Mustard	Sugarcane	Tea	Other crops
1929-30	23.89	3.50	1.1	4.54	0.63	N.A.
1930-31	24.52	3.09	1.46	4.6	0.57	N.A

Here, 1 maund = 0.037 M.T. and 1 M.T. =26.79 maund in India
(www.convertunits.com/from/maund+[India]/to/metric+tons)
Source: Ranjit Kumar Dey, *The Statistical Account of Tripura,* Uppal Publishing House, New Delhi, 2000, pp. 29-30.

The number of crops, which were specified in table no. 5.10, was not the original crops to be cultivated in Tripura in the earlier past. The crops like jute, sugarcane, mustard and pulses were not cultivated in Tripura in the earlier days. It was the result of Bengali immigrant those who introduced the crops in Tripura.[87] Mustard or oilseeds are normally used by the Bengalis as food ingredients. Hence, as the Bengali immigrants increased in Tripura the production of oilseeds was also increased. It is also noticed that the growth of rice production was increased consecutively in comparison with other crops and it was due to the influx of Bengali immigrants, for whom rice is the main food.

Jhum or shifting cultivation was a great obstacle on the way to modernisation. Hence, the rulers of Tripura who wanted to modernize the state never wanted to continue the shifting cultivation in the state, but it was not an easy task to be completed just with a single order or regulation because Jhum cultivation was the base of the Tribal lifeline. Hence, the Tribal Reserve area was made during the rule of maharaja as a part of their scheme to wean the tribals away from the practices of shifting cultivation and to settle them permanently on land.[88] The rulers of Tripura wanted to confine the shifting cultivation within the periphery of that reserved area so that the rest of the lands of the state could be made free from the evil effects of Jhum cultivation and much importance could be provided on plough cultivation. However, the reserve areas were sometimes prohibited by the Royal authority for Jhum cultivation. In the year 1939, the area of 548 sq. miles consisting of three parts of forest of Langai, Machhmara and Unokoti of Kailashahar and Dharmanagar was proclaimed as Tribal Reserved area but those areas were prohibited for Jhum cultivation.[89]

However, this Tribal reserve area for shifting cultivation was affected largely by the influx of the refugees and their rehabilitation during

---

87 *Tripura District Gazetteers*, Education Publications, Department of Education, Government of Tripura, Agartala, 1975, p. 168.

88 Bani Prasanna Misra, Op.cit.

89 Gayatri Bhattacharyya, *Op.cit*, p.126.

the Regency period (1947-1949). The Royal administration though specified the Tribal reserve areas for Jhum cultivation for the tribals but in reality, some parts of reserve areas were sacrificed in the name of modernisation and rehabilitation, which is evident from a Royal order. "By an order of the Regent dated 14.8.1948 A.D. 300 sq. miles out of 1950 sq. miles previously allotted by the orders of Late Maharaja B. B. Manikya Bahadur Memo. No. 325, dated 7th Aswin, 1353 T.E. as tribal reserve area were released for increasing land revenue, economic growth and particularly for refugee rehabilitation."[90] Accordingly, 300 sq. miles of areas which were declared as *Khas* land by the Government but previously utilized by the aborigines as Jhum cultivation land, went from their hands.

However, squeezing the tribal economy based on Jhum cultivation had a major impact on the economy of the state of Tripura. It boosts up the economic growth of the state. The agricultural economy based on shifting cultivation now began to shift towards settled or plough cultivation, which augmented the economic growth rate of the state.

The industries in the state were very much primitive in their class. In the first half of the 20th century, except tea industry, there were no other important labour-based industries in the state; rather the state depended on the cottage industries. According to the Census Bibarani 1931, "1.8 per cent of the population, except the tea garden labourers were engaged in cottage industries."[91] Among the cottage industries, maximum people of Tripura during that period were engaged in the weaving industry and a negligible amount of people were engaged in other industries (Table No. 5.11)

---

90 Ibid. p.17.

91 Takhur Shri Somendra Chandra Devbarma, *Census Bibarani* (Bengali), 1340 T.E., Tribal Research and Cultural Institute, Government of Tripura, Agartala, p. 101.

Table 5.11.

Number of people engaged in industries in Tripura (1931)

Industries	Number of people engaged
Weaving Industry	5,409
Timber Industry	299
Metal Industry	66
Pottery	28
Chemical goods Industry	12
Food Industry	292
Clothes & cosmetic Industry	425
House building	96
Vehicle Industry	1
Others	18

Source: Takhur Shri Somendra Chandra Devbarma, *Census Bibarani* (Bengali), 1340 T.E., Tribal Research and Cultural Institute, Government of Tripura, Agartala, p. 101.

Another industrial sector is the Tea industry, which was purely dominated by immigrants. The owners of those Tea gardens were Bengalis while its labourers were immigrant tribes. The local tribes among the tea garden labourers are very negligible.[92]

The communication systems of Tripura in the first phase (1901-1947) of the present study were very primitive and undeveloped. Capital Agartala had no permanent road links with the other subdivisions of the state. Hence, the movements of the people were very rare except for the royal officials and traders. Externally, Tripura used to maintain good open relations with Calcutta, Dacca, and many other adjoining districts of British Bengal. The traders frequently used the roads, railways, rivers of British Bengal and

---

92 P.N. Bhattadherjee & Ram Gopal Singh, *Tea Plantation and the Tribes of Tripura,* Tripura State Tribal Cultural Research Institute and Museum, Government of Tripura, Agartala, 1995, p. 59.

the port of Chittagong. Nevertheless, due to the partition of India, the adjoining territories of Tripura went to Pakistan and Tripura became a land lock territory. Partition of India made the communication between West Bengal and Tripura much harder.

Chapter VI

Epilogue

Economic disparities are generally considered as the major cause of migration though other powerful powers like political, social, environmental factors, criminal and ethnic violence etc. are also responsible for migration. It is evident that push and pulls factors of migration are generally motivated by economic imbalance. It is also true that the way through which an underdeveloped state provoked immigration may be a cause of emigration from that particular state.

Now when the matter of the relationship between migration and development comes then the question general arise whether migrants are an indispensable part of the developmental process of a state. As we know that all countries have their own social, political and economic base on which the structure of development is framed. Hence, once again a question arises that what will be the determining factor to consider a state as developed and underdeveloped. Also, it is evident from the previous chapter that controversy still remains among scholars regarding the nature of the migration-development relationship.

Hence, to determine the migration development nexus in the princely hilly state of Tripura, the first thing that we have to determine is the developmental structure of Tripura in the period under review. Though it is not possible to determine the exact height of development it was true that Tripura before her amalgamation with Indian Union was a princely state with her stagnant, semi-feudal and self-sufficient hill economy based on shifting cultivation. The market economy was never encouraged by the earlier Manikya rulers and was unknown to those tribal rural people of Hill

Tripura. In fact, the economy of the region was about in the subsistence level and the surplus production was extremely limited. Consequently, when the rulers of Tripura began to modernize their state and wanted to make it up to date, they had to depend on the immigrants, both educated and uneducated but skilled labourers.

As we know that Tripura is surrounded by Bengal and the rulers of Tripura had always maintained a close nexus with the state. Therefore, educated and elite Bengali people as well as uneducated but skilled labourers immigrated into the state. Factually, it is true that the migrants are often the most risk-taking and self-motivated members of the society and thus, migrants always underpinned economic growth, nation-building and enriched cultures. Therefore, the Bengali people who were self-motivated and gave the response to the invitation of the rulers of Tripura to immigrate were ready to take the risk and hence, development was the usual consequence. The increase of revenue in the Royal treasury, improvement in the field of education, health, trade, agriculture, etc. in the 1st half of the 20th century, was the result of Bengali immigrants into Tripura. The rulers of Tripura pulled the elites as well as the plough cultivators of Bengal. The rulers of Tripura provided all sorts of facilities to those immigrants.

The state economy was boosted up by the Bengali immigrants. Plough cultivation took place instead of shifting or Jhum cultivation, the only major agricultural source of hill Tripura. As a result, the state revenue increased enormously. The net area showed an increase in Tripura during the period under study. In sectors like communication, health, education, trade there were signs of progress and it was only due to Bengali immigrants.

Therefore, after analysing the development of the state during the period under study it is evident that Tripura was totally a changed state. She left her age-old primitive agriculture-based rural economy and advanced towards a modern agricultural and urban-based economy. The full credit of transferring Tripura into a modern era goes to those immigrant Bengalis.

The flow of modernisation was not concentrated only in the urban areas as the immigrants in a large number also settled themselves in the rural and hilly regions of the state. Hence, the wave of modernisation also affected the aborigines living in the interior of hill Tripura.

Tripura had a motionless, semi-feudal and subsistence economy. She never experienced the suffocation of economic shortfall. There was neither the pressure of population on land nor the pressure of unemployment on the social-economic structure. As the rulers of Tripura wanted to modernize their state based on their own culture and tradition, the economic development of their state was thus a part of their modernisation process and to fulfil that part they invited the Bengalis from Bengal and paved the way for the Bengalis to migrate into Tripura.

In the last part of the Manikya rule, along with a large number of Bengali elites as well as illiterate Bengali peasants, a quantitative number of the tribal population from various parts of India immigrated to Tripura. Those immigrants were considered economic migrants. The people who immigrated to Tripura during that period do not belong to the same economic background.

Scarcity of jobs, food, lack of proper respect in the society led to such migration. Again, on some occasions the people who wanted to exploit the situation and to take full advantage of the economic backwardness of an underdeveloped region migrate into those areas. They intend to regulate the economy of those underdeveloped areas and to make an ultimate benefit of their own and Tripura was no exception. Under the guidance of able Bengali administrators and skilled immigrant communities, the tea industry flourished in the state and arrange for a major share in the state revenue.

Hence, it can be said that immigration and development in Tripura are very much interlinked with each other. The influx of immigrants in Tripura brought enthusiasm to the State developmental process. Modernisation of economic transactions spread into the remote interior regions, which is in itself a great economic advance. The patterns of the demands of those tribal people were changed significantly. The Bengali immigrants are educated and refined people and thus they provided an assured supply of skilled and semi-skilled labourers in agriculture and teachers, doctors and other professional personnel and without their contribution modern Tripura could not be built. It was the immigrants, which has been the source of supply of whatever entrepreneurial talent that helped socio-economic development in the state and brought further development in this direction. The literate persons among them are fit for white-collar jobs. Accordingly, every sector is being developed by its endeavour. However, the fruits of development are, of course, is shared both by the immigrants and the aborigines though may not be on an equal footing.

Therefore, it became clear that the immigrants played a vital role in the developmental process of Tripura in the first half of the 20th century. Now the question which generally arises in the mind of the scholars that whether under-developmental factors of the state of origin is responsible for migration? In the case of Tripura, the answer is very critical. As we know the people who immigrated to Tripura during the period under study are maximum from colonial Bengal and some others from the other part of British India. It is also true that from the socio-economic perspective the Princely state Tripura was much underdeveloped in comparison to Colonial India, especially from Bengal. Though socio-economic disturbances are some of the causes of immigration into Tripura but the theory of immigration of moving the immigrants from underdeveloped areas to a developed one don't suit the immigration scenario of Tripura. Also, the development of the place of origin due to emigration is also not suited in the case of the migration process in Tripura. As we know that the immigrants who came to Tripura except for the "Ziratia" peasants and a marginal section of peasants' cultivators, maximum of those immigrants settled permanently into Tripura. Hence, here the benefit goes to the hoist nation i.e. Tripura and not the place of origin i.e. colonial India. It can be said in this context that it is not necessary for economic migration that the migrants will move only from an underdeveloped area to a developed one for their livelihood. Economic migration depends on the economic status of that particular migrant in the place of its origin rather than on the economic conditions of that host place or state.

Therefore, we can say that there was a close nexus between the whole migration process and developmental activities during the period under study. The road of modern Tripura which was once dreamt by the rulers was started during that period and the reflection of modernisation in Tripura was clearly visible only due to the influx of immigrants, those who with their best efforts and potential laid the foundation of modern Tripura.

Bibliography

Primary Source

1. *Census Bibarani 1340 T.E. (1931 A.D)*, Tribal Research and Cultural Institute, Government of Tripura, Agartala, 1997.

2. *Census of India 1961, Demographic and Socio-Economic Profiles of the Hill Areas of North-East India.* Office of The Registrar General, India, Ministry of Home Affairs, New Delhi.

3. *Census of India 1961*, Vol. XXVI, Tripura, District Census Handbook, Section – I, C.R.Paul, Government of Tripura, Government Printing and Stationary Department, Agartala, 1964,

4. *Census of India, 1901*, Vol.VI, The Lower Provinces of Bengal and their feudatories, Part I, The Report, Bengal Secretariat Press, Calcutta, 1902

5. Census of India, 1951, Vol. I, India, Part II-A – Demographic Tables, Govt. of India Press, Delhi, 1955

6. Census of India, 1951, Vol. XII, Assam, Manipur and Tripura, Part IA, Report, Shillong, 1954.

7. Census of India, 1951, Vol. XII, Assam, Manipur and Tripura, Part IA, Report, Shillong, 1954,

8. Census Report 1310 T.E. (1901 A.D.), Tribal Research Institute, Government of Tripura, Agartala, Re-printing 1995

9. Eastern Bengal and Assam District Gazetteers, Noakhali, Allahabad, 1911.

10. Eastern Bengal District Gazetteer, Tipperah, Allahabad, 1910

11. Geographical and Statistical Report Of The District of Tipperah (Robert B. Smart), Bengal Secretariat Office, Calcutta, 1866

12. Imperial Gazetteers of India. Vol.XIII, (New Edition), Oxford, London, 1908.

13. Memoranda on the Indian State, 1932, Government of India, Central Publication Branch, Calcutta, 1933.

14. Statistical Account of Bengal, (W.W.Hunter) Vol. VI, London, 1876 (1973 Reprint).

15. Tripura a portrait of population, Census of India 1971, Published by Controller of Publications, Civil lines, Delhi, 1975

16. Tripura District Gazetteers, Government of Tripura, Agartala, 1975.

17. Tripura Rajye Tirish Bochor (Thirty Years in Tripura), Dharmanagar Division, (In Bengali), Education Directorate, Government of Tripura, Agartala, 1972.

18. Tripura State Gazette Sankalan (1903-1949), Director of Education, Government of Tripura, November, 1971,

19. Tripura State Gazette, 30th Agrahayana, 1326 T.E. Agartala

20. Tripura State Gazetteer (Special Edition) 1355 T.E. Agartala

Secondary Source

1. Adhikari O.S., Four Immigrant Tribes of Tripura, Directorate of Research Tribal Welfare Department, Government of Tripura, Agartala, 1988

2. Bareh Hamlet, Encyclopedia of North-East India: Vol. VIII, Tripura, Mittal Publications, Delhi, 2007

3. Barua Debapriya Deb, Treatise on Traditional Social Institution of the 'Tripuri' Community, Directorate of Research, Government of Tripura, Agartala, 1983

4. Bhattacharjee J. B. (ed.), Sequences of Development in North East India, Omsons Publications, New Delhi, 1989

5. Bhattacharjee Pravas Ranjan, Economic Transition in Tripura, Vikas Publishing House Pvt. Ltd., New Delhi, 1993

6. Bhattacharjee S.R., Tribal Insurgency in Tripura, Inter-India Publications, New Delhi, 1989

7. Bhattacharjee Suchintya, Genesis of Tribal Extremism in Tripura, Gyan Books Pvt. Ltd. New Delhi, 1991

8. Bhattacharyya A. C., Progressive Tripura, Inter-India Publications, New Delhi, Reprint- 1985

9. Bhattacharyya Banikantha, Tripura Administration The Era of Modernisation, Mittal Publications, Delhi, 1986

10. 10.Bhattacherjee P. N . & Singh Ram Gopal, Tea Plantation and the Tribes of Tripura, Tripura State Tribal Cultural Research Institute and Museum, Govt. of Tripura, Agartala, 1995

11. Bhowmik Dwijendralal, Tribal Religion of Tripura – A Socio-Religious Analysis, Tribal Research Institute, Government of Tripura, Agartala, 2003

12. Bianchini Stefano, Chaturvedi Sanjay, Ivekovic Rada and Samaddar Ranabir, Partitions – Reshaping states and minds, Taylor & Francis e- Library, 2006

13. Bikram-Kisor Kumar Sahadev (Maharaj), Chaudhuri Jagadis Gan, Tripura – Historical Documents, Firma Klm Private Limited, Calcutta, 1994

14. Biswas Prasenjit, Thomas C. Joshua, Peace in India's North-East: Meaning, Metaphor, and Method : Essays of Concern and Commitment, Regency Publications, Indian Council of Social Science Research. North Eastern Regional Centre, Shillong

15. Brownmiller Susan, Against Our Will: Men, Women and Rape, Ballantine Books, Fawcett Columbine, New York, June 1993

16. Butalia Urvashi, The Other Side of Silence – Voices from the Partition of

17. India, Penguin Books India Pvt. Ltd, New Delhi, 1998 17.Chakraborty Dipannita, Land Question in Tripura, Akansha Publishing House, New Delhi, 2004

18. Chakravarti Mahadev, Admisistration Reports of Tripura State, since 1902, Vol. 1, Gyan Publishing House, New Delhi, 1994, 19.Chandha Vivek (Lt Col), Low Intensity Conflicts in India – An Analysis, Sage Publications, New Delhi, 2005

19. Chatterjee Jaya, *The Spoils of Partition, Bengal and India, 1947 – 1967*, Cambridge University Press, New York, 2007

20. Chaudhuri Jagadis Gan, *The Reangs of Tripura*, Directorate of Research, Department of Welfare of Sch. Tribes and Sch Castes, Government of Tripura, 1983

21. Chaudhury Asusua Basu Roy, Dey Ishita, *Citizens, Non-Citizens, and the Camps Lives,*Mahanirban Calcutta Research Group, Kolkata, 2009

22. Cholewinski Ryszard, Guchteneire Paul De and Pecoud Antoine (ed.), *Migration and Human Rights, The United Nations*

Convention on Migrant Workers' Rights, Cambridge University Press, Cambridge, 2009

23. Choudhuri Dipak Kumar, *Reflection on the History of Tripura*, Kalyanbrata Chakraborty on behalf of Bhasa, Agartala, January, 2006

24. Cumming J.G., I.C.S. *Settlement Officer, Survey and Settlement of the*

25. *Chakla Roshnabad Estate in the Districts of Tippera and Noakhali, 1892-99*, Tripura State Tribal Cultural Research Institute & Museum, Government of Tripura, Agartala, December, 1997.

26. De Nilanjan, *A Historical Analysis of Migration in Tripura : 1900-1971*, Research India Publications, New Delhi, 2014

27. De Sibopada , *Migrations and the North-East*, Anamika Publishers & Distributors (P) Ltd., New Delhi, 2005.

28. Dev Varman S.B.K., *A Study over the Jhum and Jhumia Rehabilitation in the Union Territory of Tripura*. Directorate of Research, Department of Welfare for Sch. Tribes & Sch. Castes, Government of Tripura, Agartala, 1999

29. Dey Ranjit Kumar, *The Statistical Account of Tripura*, Uppal Publishing House, New Delhi, 2000

30. Dubey S.M (ed.), *North East India – A Sociological Study*, Concept Publishing Company, Delhi, 1978

31. Ganguli J.B., *The Benign Hills*, Tripura Darpan Prakashani, Agartala, March 1983.

32. Ganguly J.B, , *Economic Problems of the Jhumias of Tripura*, Bookland Private Ltd., Calcutta-6, 1969

33. Ganguly J.B., *Economic Problems Of The Jhumias Of Tripura*, Bookland Private Ltd. Calcutta, 1969.

34. Ganguly Jalad Baran, *An Economic History of North East India, 1826 to 1947*, Akansha Publishing House, New Delhi, 2006.

35. Gopal S., *Selected Works of Jawaharlal Nehru, Vol. XIV*, Part I, New Delhi, 1992

36. Gorden Marshal, Dictionary of Sociology, OUP, Oxford and New York,1998

37. Guha Samar, East Bengal Minorities Since Delhi Pact, All Parties Minorities' Rights Council, 1953

38. Guha Thakurta S.N., India – The land and the people – Tripura, Director National Book Trust, India, New Delhi, 1999 (2nd Edition)

39. Gupta U.N., Human Rights, Vol. III, Atlantic Publishers &Distributors,New Delhi, 2006

40. Hasan Mushirul (ed.), India's Partition: Process, Strategy and Mobilisation, Oxford University Press, New Delhi, 2003

41. Hassan Mohammad Izhar, Population Geography, Rawat Publications, Jaipur, 2005

42. Hay Jeff, The Partition of British India, Chelsea House Publishers, New York, 2006

43. Kamra A. J., The Prolonged partition and its Pogroms: Testimonies on Violence Against Hindus in East Bengal 1946-64, Voice of India, New Delhi, 2000

44. Kanwal Gurmeet, V.K. Shrivastava, Defenders of the dawn: a panorama of Eastern Command, Lancer Publisher, New Delhi, 2000

45. Kumar B.B. (ed.), Illegal Migration from Bangladesh, Concept Publishing Company, New Delhi, 2006

46. Mahto Kailash, Population Mobility and Economic Development In Eastern India, Inter-India Publications, New Delhi, 1985

47. Malla N. (ed), Nationalism, Regionalism and Philosophy of National Integration, Regency Publication, New Delhi, 1998

48. Menon V.P., The Story of the Integration of The Indian States, Orient Longmans Limited, Bombay, Reprint- 1969

49. Michael J. Piore, Birds of Passage: Migrant Labor in Industrial Societies, Cambridge University Press, Cambridge, 1979

50. Misra Bani Prasanna, Socioeconomic Adjustments of Tribals: Case-Study of Tripura Jhumias, People's Publishing House, New Delhi, 1976.

51. Mohanta Bijon, Tripura in the Light of Socio-Political Movements since 1945, Progressive Publishers, Kolkata, February, 2004.

52. Mookerjee Syama Prasad, Leves from a diary. Oxford University Pres. New Delhi, 1993

53. Proceedings of North East India History Association, Fifth Session, Aizawl, 1984

54. Rachardson W.Harry, Elements of Regional Economics, Pengwin Books Ltd. Harmondinath, Midle Sex, England, 1970 (Reprint)

55. Ray S. C., Land Revenue Administration in India, Calcutta University, 1915

56. Saigal Omesh, Tripura: its History and Culture, Concept Publishing Company, Dehli, 1978

57. Samaddar Ranabir (ed.), Refugees and the State : Practices of Asylum and Care in India, 1947-2000, Sage Publications, New Delhi, 2003

58. Sen Tripur Chandra, Tripura in Transition (1923-1957 A.D.), Self Publication, Agartala, Tripura, 1970

59. Shimray U A, Devi M D Usha, Trends and Patterns of Migration: Interface with Education – A Case of the North-Eastern Region, Institute for Social and Economic Change, Bangalore, 2009

60. Sisson Richard, Leo E.Rose, War and Secession, Pakistan, India and the creation of Bangladesh, University of California Press Ltd., Oxford, England, 1990

61. Skeldon R., Migration and Development: A Global Perspective, Essex: Addison Wesley, Longman, Harlow, 1997

62. Srivastava S.C, Demographic Profile of North East India, Mittal Publications, Dehli, 1987

63. Thomas C Joshua (ed.), Dimensions of Displaced People in North-East India, Regency Publications, New Delhi, 2002

64. Thomas Faist, Margit Fauser, and Peter Kivisto (ed), The Migration-Development Nexus: A Transnational Perspective, Palgrave Macmillan, UK, 2011

65. Valtonen Kathleen, Social Work and Migration, Immigrant and Refugee Settlement and Integration, Ashgate Publishing Limited, England, 2008

66. Vernat Jaques , The Refugee in the Post World War, George Allen and Unwin Ltd., London, 1953

67. Weiner, Myron, The Global Migration Crisis: Challenge to States and to Human Rights, Harper Collings College, Publishers: New York, 1995.

68. Zamindar Vazira Fazila-Yacoobali, The Long Partition and the making of Modern South Asia Refugees, Boundaries, Histories, Viking by Penguin Books India , New Delhi, 2008

Personal Interview

1. Sunil Krishna Paul, retired T.C.S. Officer (1995) and former Assistant Survey Officer (North and South district of Tripura) in 1971, Dharmanagar.

Journals

1. Center for Spatially Integrated Social Science, 1885, http://www.csiss.org/classics/content/90

2. Demography, Vol.3, No. 1, 1966

3. Economic and Political Weekly, August 30, 2008

4. ESD. 83 – Fall 2001, Online journal http://web.mit.edu/esd.83/www/notebook/WorldSystem.pdf.

5. Far Eastern Economic Review, 28 August, 1971

6. Folklore and Folkloristics, Vol.2; No.1, June 2009

7. Frontiers In Demographic Economics, Vol. 75, No. 2, May 1985

8. Global Migration Perspectives, No. 50, October 2005

9. Human Architecture: Journal of the Sociology of Self-Knowledge, VII,

10. Fall 2009,5-14

11. International Migration Review, Vol. 26, No. 2, Special Issue: The New Europe and International Migration, Summer 1

12. International Migration Review, Voll. 34, No. 4, Winter, 2000

13. International Migration Review, Voll.11, No.2, Summer 1977.

14. International Review of Social History, Vol. 46, 2001

15. International Social Science Journal, Vol. 52, 2000

16. Journal of Borderlands Studies, Volume 21, No. 1, Spring 2006

17. Journal of Genocide Research, 5(1), 2003

18. Journal of Human Ecology, volume 7, Number 3, July, 1996

19. Journal of Refugee Studies Vol. 22, No 1, 2009, Oxford University Press

Webpages

1. http://bengalvoice.blogspot.com/http://courses.washington.edu/setclass/w513_10/readings/massey1994.p

2. http://dailyinfopages.com/definition-of-migration/

3. http://dictionary.cambridge.org/dictionary/british/eco-nomic-migrant

4. http://en.wikipedia.org/wiki/Political_migration

5. http://en.wikisource.org/wiki/Resignation_letter_of_Jogendra_Nath_Mandal   http://pune.gov.in/puneCollectorate/Gazette/Poona- II/agri_experimental_gardens

6. http://www.educationforallinindia.com/page172.html.

7. http://www.enotes.com/topic/Tripura_Merger_Agreement.

8. http://www.journalarchive.jst.go.jp/jnlpdf.php?cdjournal=jjasas1989&cdvol=2000&noissue=12&startpage=73&chr=en

9. www.iussp2005.princeton.edu/download.aspx?submissionID=52236

10. www.ncbi.nlm.nih.gov/pubmed/12347965.

11. www.repository.forcedmigration.org/pdf/?pid=fmo:1801.

12. www.sasnet.lu.se/EASASpapers/33AnasuaBasuray.pdf.

13. http://www.businessdictionary.com/definition/development.html

14. http://www.cgdev.org/blog/what-development

15. http://globalstudies.unc.edu/files/2013/11/Hennings-Mattis-Migration-and-Development.pdf

16. https://heindehaas.files.wordpress.com/2015/05/de-haas-2007-comcad-wp-migration-and-development-theory.pdf